Molloy's Popularity Game

by

John T. Molloy

First edition

ISBN: 978-0-578-20132-0

Printed in the United States of America
JTM Publishing

TO

Maureen, Rob, Andrea

PREFACE

This book was originally designed for business people who believe others have received promotions they deserved. There are two reasons for this, if a man or woman is popular they are more likely to be thought of as smart and able and second, research shows most managers are more likely to give a raise or promotion to a popular candidate over one who is not. So chances are you did not get that job, raise or promotion you deserved because you were not as likeable as the person who did. This text is designed to make you popular which would give you the popularity advantage. In addition, this text is designed to teach people who would rather text than talk social skills they have not developed, as well as teach youngsters to be popular so that they will not bully or be bullied. When some colleges find on your school record that you bullied anyone many will not even read your application even if you're a star athlete. It has happened to thousands already and it's happening to more every day.

If you are in junior high or High School stop reading and arrange for a parent or responsible adult to spend the next several weeks with you while you read the book aloud. That will substantially increase your chances of becoming popular. If you cannot arrange for a responsible adult to work with you, you can do it on your own but it will be harder and it will take longer. If you decide to work with your children do not do so until you finished your training it is most often counterproductive.

We found explaining the techniques we use to train people and the research behind them is effective when dealing with business people but not with teenagers. Which means students do not have to read through the book before starting. As I stated earlier this book was originally designed for executives who had not received promotions they thought they deserved. However, if you read the next several pages you will think this text was designed exclusively for teenagers and young adults. The reason is we found if you do not talk directly to teenagers and young adults in the beginning of a text they are likely to think the text is not for them. Another reason is young adults usually don't have to work as hard or as long to change their signals because they are not as well ingrained. The practice times I give will work for most 13 and 14 year olds and some college students. As a general rule the older you are the harder you have to work to break ingrained habits. However, in the course on which this book is based my only recommendation was to work as long and as hard as necessary to change your negative messages into positive ones and that remains the rule.

Some teenagers have habits that make them unpopular that are as hard to break as those of 50 and 60 year old olds which will make it necessary for them to practice for weeks or months to change a single habitual mistake. While almost 30% of adult men and 50% of adult women can go through the entire program correcting every negative signal easily within 2 to 3 months most take longer. There are a few who will complete the course in a shorter period of time. While you might be one of those fortunate ones, I do not suggest you start unless you are ready to spend four hours a week for the next three to six months. Nevertheless, I start by giving the time necessary for 13 and14 year olds to change their ingrained signals. The reason is simple, you need a place to start.

The primary reason there are no specific limitations on time or effort is the task is so complex. In order to be popular you must change signals that you've been sending all your life. If you are in the habit of slouching when you meet people it is relatively easy to just stand erect on those occasions.

The problem is you often forget when actually meeting people, so you continue to slouch. If over and over you say to yourself, when greeting people stand up straight, when greeting people stand up straight, that thought will most likely pop into your mind when you first meet people and on those occasions you will stand up straight. Problem solved, yes and no. We found that most people when they stand ramrod straight change the expression on their faces. It often goes from friendly and relaxed to authoritarian and sometimes angry. To appear friendly, you must then change a second signal which can require another change, and so forth. I never said this course would be easy, it isn't, for most it is difficult and requires hard work.

The quickest study I ever ran across was a man in his early 50s who was given an early copy of my texts and went through it in less than 25 minutes. He was a speed reader. After that short period of time he did everything right, he stood up straight, put a small understated smile on his face, leaned in slightly and charmed almost everyone he met . He is the exception that proves the rule. After teaching this course for many years I know those who complete it in two or three months are moving at lightning speed. Less than 1% of my students finished a course in less than 2 weeks for the rest of us it will take substantially longer and it is neither quick nor easy.

There seems to be a compensating factor. I met that very talented speed reader four years later and he said he had received two promotions he would never have received without my training. However, he was still working on three minor mistakes he kept making. When someone changes ingrained hard to change signals that made them unpopular to new ones that make them charming, they often become ingrained and difficult to change. As a result, the old signals that made them unpopular hardly ever recurred.

Popularity is a very complicated subject and the way you approach it will depend on your individual needs. However, at the same time it's rather a simple subject because the same signals that a teenage boy or girl can send to their classmates to charm them will work with 45 and 50 year old executives. Once you learn to be popular with your own group you can charm almost anyone. That is why I would like everyone to read the complete text, even those sections that seem to have nothing to do with them. As you move through the course, some of the seemingly useless information you will find helpful. So read on.

You should start working on improving your popularity skills by following the directions carefully and in the order in which they are given eg. rereading and memorizing sections as directed. It will not be easy but it will be the most rewarding thing you have ever done. Good luck!

* * * * * * * * * * * *

Join a popularity group at work or at school. If one does not exist, start one. If a friend wants to join but doesn't have a book, he can as long as you're willing to loan them your book and let him read the appropriate chapter.

INTRODUCTION

The reason this book is called "Molloy's Popularity Game" is we wanted our readers to know if they understood that learning to be popular was similar to learning to play golf or tennis they were more likely to succeed. As with golf and tennis you cannot expect to read a book and then go out and play like a pro and you cannot simply read this book and become instantly popular. If you wish to be a better golfer or tennis player you hire a pro who studies your game, points out your mistakes and helps you correct them. This text will act as your popularity pro, it will show you how to identify your flaws and through practice correct them. If you are willing to spend the time and effort necessary to improve your golf, tennis or popularity game you'll become a better player. With golf and tennis, you'll become a winner on the links or on the court but with popularity you'll become a winner in life. If you want to play the popularity game like a pro, read on.

If you are an adult working with a youngster you should do so at the kitchen table. Since I insist that every student read aloud you can work with him in his room but you must stay with him. There is overwhelming statistical evidence that when a parent sits with their child that child learns more and more quickly. That is why when training young people to be popular I strongly recommend that a responsible adult work with them for at least the first six to eight weeks. To be specific if a child does their homework where they are being monitored by their parents their marks in most cases will go up a full grade. If the parent sits and works with them their marks usually goes up a grade to a grade and a half and sometimes more. This approach to education became standard among Oriental mothers whose children are now found in significant numbers in America's top universities and the scientific community. These students once out of school earn 30 or 40% more than the average American college graduate.

At this point your question is or should be, who are you and what makes you an expert on popularity. My name is John T Molloy and I'm the author of the Dress for Success books, Live for Success, How to Work the Competition into the Ground and Have Fun Doing It, and Why Men Marry Some Women and Not Others, to name just a few of my books. The last book was designed to help women get the man they want to marry them. That may not be politically correct these days but it was translated into 24 languages and distributed in over 145 countries. I also had nationally syndicated programs on success on ABC and NBC radio for over 12 years and I wrote a column for 30 years which was distributed by the New York Times and the LA Times.

More importantly I have been running a sales and popularity course for clients for almost 35 years. While I started training salesmen to charm buyers when they walked into their offices, over the years I transitioned into training salespeople who worked with clients and had to be charming all the time, to executives and finally the general public.

THEY WOULD RATHER TEXT THAN TALK

Although, there is no single term for them today. their existence is recognized by industry and academia. I've heard them referred to as iphone idiots, smartphone dummies, smartphone zombies and so forth. I interviewed men and women in corporations who hired people while they were still in school. The first thing I tell anyone who has a smartphone is to turn it off if you're going to an interview. When I questioned corporate recruiters who worked on campuses they told me one story after another about how poorly some of today's college graduates communicate in person. The people I interviewed often started with, "you won't believe this but I've had more than one student tell me to hold on while he answered his phone." Another college recruiter, as I walked into the area where he was interviewing pointed at a young man and said that idiot with a 3.8 index in chemical engineering was texting in his pocket during the interview. Before he arrived I was ready to give him a signing bonus, now I wouldn't touch him with a ten-foot pole.

The young people I have just described are either stupid, rude or both while most young people who live on their smartphones are neither. However, companies are still reluctant to hire them. Several recruiters told me that if they saw a young person walk up to their booth texting and the minute the interview was over walk away texting, it made them nervous.

Many business people believe that young people today do not have the social skills that their older brother's or father's had at the same age. A substantial percentage never connect socially with their coworkers and as a result they are not part of any team effort. When you put them in a department rather than adding to that section's team spirit and productivity they subtract from it.

The academic community recognizes the problem as well. I spoke to dozens of teachers both in high school and college and they said that at times they knew students in class were texting rather than paying attention. Many of the older and more experienced teachers thought that some of today's students were less social than their counterparts were 20 years ago. A professor at MIT who retired just a few years ago said that he believed it impacted the creativity of the students. As he saw it face to face communication encouraged creativity. He said 30 years ago MIT was a petri dish for new ideas. Students not only had all night study sessions they had all night bull sessions. Although most of the time they produced nothing but bleary eyed students some of them produced breakthroughs, new thinking that turned into doctoral theses, patents, and more than one multimillion-dollar Industry. When he questioned the students who sat in on those very productive bull sessions and asked them why they thought they produced creative ideas while others didn't, their answers surprised him. He thought they would say they cooperated with each other but most of them said they were competing with the same people with whom they were cooperating. They left those sessions with the intention of being the first to prove this or that worked or didn't work or to turn theoretical ideas into practical products. He said that is not happening today because texting does not have the emotional impact of the old fashioned bull session. In addition, for some reason today's MIT students are more interested in marks than ideas.

It may sound as if I'm against those who text all the time, I'm not, it's part of our 21st century culture. In fact, unless you use your smartphone efficiently you can't possibly understand the 21st century, or participate in it in a meaningful way. Nevertheless, learning to communicate effectively in person is necessary for business and social success.

Which leads us to how to go about reading this very unusual book. If you are a student you should ignore the first suggestion. You are already working on improving your popularity skills by following the directions in this book eg. rereading and memorizing sections as directed. We found explaining the techniques we use to train people and the research behind them is effective when dealing with business people but not with teenagers. Teenagers do not have to read through the book before starting.

First, if you are an adult start by reading the entire book as if it were a regular book. While doing that ignore all directions to reread some sections and memorize others. What the book will tell you is why I repeat information and insist you read sections over and over. If my methodology makes sense to you it will make doing it easier and you will progress more quickly.

Second, ask yourself do I have the equipment necessary to follow the instructions in this book. If not, purchase that equipment.

Third, decide if you are going to work by yourself or with a group. You can change your mind anytime you wish. If you load the book onto your youngsters cell phone they will automatically share with their friends and probably form groups to work together. Remember they live on their cell phones.

Fourth, whether you're working by yourself or with a group you are going to have to set aside a minimum of 4 hours a week to videotape, analyze your errors, and work at correcting them. Will your present schedule allow you to do this and if not what changes must be made in your schedule. If you cannot fit the work required into your present schedule you can start on your own but it will take more time for you to reach your goal. Keep in mind there is a drawback to working on your own, often students are not able to pick out their own flaws and as a result they waste time doing the wrong exercises.

Fifth, after you finish the first section of this text follow our instructions in the order in which they are given. Do not skip ahead to a section or sections you think will help you. This book is based on years of trial and error and most importantly, it works. Books have been written before that promised to make you popular but they never delivered. If you were unpopular before you read those books in all probability you were unpopular after you read them. This book is different, it will make almost everyone who works with it more popular. Whether you find it difficult to make and keep friends or have no problem making friends, you will find you will be able to charm people you were never able to charm before and because of that your life will change for the better. I realize I am asking you for a major commitment in time and effort but it is necessary not only if you want to succeed socially and in business but to get along with most of the people you meet.

If you wish to be popular the first thing you have to do is discover the everyday you, how you appear to others when you are with individuals, groups, by yourself, reading, working, watching television, walking along the street, and so forth. You can work alone but you will learn more quickly if you work with others. If you work by yourself you have to set up a camera on a tripod and videotape yourself for at least a week. These tapes will be most useful if you videotape yourself when interacting with others. The most effective way of getting pictures of you interacting with others is to use a cell phone. In one section I describe how to do that so I'm not going into more detail here. Of course it is easier if you have your mate, a friend or a popularity partner tape you.

When you have at least 20 hours of videotape, examine them carefully and you will probably see how you look most of the time. Once again this is difficult to accomplish on your own but it can be done. The best way to do this is to get someone who knows you very well to look at the videos and to pick out the one or ones they see as the real you. Over half of you will find that there are several versions of the real you. That is not good, particularly if you are a woman. Popular people usually look more or less the same all the time and since a consistent message tells the world you are not a phony and can be trusted, it is absolutely critical if you wish to be popular.

If you are working on your own you will probably have to guess which one is the likable you. Most of us do not see ourselves as the world sees us, so guessing is not a very effective method. The best way to find out which version of you is seen as likable is to run a simple test. Have someone who knows you well look at the tapes and choose the picture or pictures they see in their mind when they close their eyes and think about how you look. If they see more than one version of you have 10 others who are not your friends rate them on a 1 to 10 basis with 10 being the most likable. If a picture gets a 9 or a 10 use that one as your model. Once you discover the most likable you take that picture and put it next to every mirror you own.

If no version of you tests as likeable go to a mirror and try to put on the face that appears most often. Once you find that face, put on a small smile or pre-smile. That is the look you put on your face just as you are about to smile. Stand just a bit straighter and at the same time make any additional adjustment you think makes you look more pleasant. Take a picture of that look and show it to your friends or even better strangers. If they agree you look pleasant put that picture on those mirrors, if not go back to the mirror and try again. Once you have a picture that is seen as friendly, practice becoming that person, until you get it down pat. I don't know how long that will take it depends on you, but keep practicing until that person becomes the real you.

If you are a teenager put that picture on your phone and ask your friends if they think you look friendly and approachable. Only ask those who are really your friends and you trust. Ask for that help and once you have that friendly picture on your phone glance at it regularly until it becomes the real you. This will take weeks or months.

That's a far bigger job than you think. There are a number of reasons that is so difficult, the primary one is the picture on the front of this book. It is my picture when I was three, in those days they dressed children differently so I may look younger. (PLACE PICTURE HERE) The critical discovery that dictates most of what we do in this book is most children develop the face and the body language that they will carry for the rest of their lives when they are about two years of age. I'm sure you know most babies look almost the same and then they become real people, that is because they copy a family member or friend. Most of them adjust their look as they grow, particularly young women as they enter puberty. However, since their popularity primarily depends on how they look, a decision made when they were two often determines how popular they are now and will be for the rest of their lives. I know that is not fair but neither is life. If you wish to become more popular you are going to have to change that look and the message it sends. The way you hold your body and your facial muscles are well ingrained habits that will take effort, personal commitment and a plan to change. As a result of 25+ years of trial and error testing we have that plan.

The second reason it is more difficult than you think is we are all creatures of habit. No matter how hard you try, no matter how long you practice you will occasionally slip back into old habits, so you have to constantly monitor your behavior by regularly videotaping and correcting flaws when you find them.

REREAD THE ABOVE TWO PARAGRAPHS PREFERABLY ALOUD AT LEAST 3X

If you want to make a good first impression you should put a small friendly smile or pre-smile on your face. Then smile just a bit more and lean slightly forward or back if you are very tall, large or for any reason intimidating when shaking hands, holding onto the person's hand a second or two longer than you usually do. As soon as you're finished shaking hands smoothly without hesitating move back so that you are no longer invading the personal space of the person you just met. This is almost a foolproof formula for making a good first impression.

READ THE ABOVE PARAGRAPH OVER AND OVER UNTIL YOU HAVE IT MEMORIZED.

Once you have it memorized repeat it 7X a day for the next week or until you are so familiar with the material you can repeat it word for word anytime day or night Then reread it aloud at least 5X a day for the next three months. These steps must become part of your DNA, so they pop into your mind no matter how much pressure you are under. When they do you will make a good first impression every time.

This is the only how to book ever designed by those who have read early versions of the text. Because this book was designed by students who took my popularity course I repeat myself, tell you to read paragraphs and sometimes sections several times and insist that you memorize parts of this book so that you can repeat them instinctively. That is very hard work and will take time and effort but it is the only way you will learn to turn your charm off and on like a lightbulb and to become really popular. It is the reason this book is only one third the size of the original draft because my students told me to cut out anything that they didn't think was necessary. Those who read my earlier books know they are filled with research and data, my students told me to remove any discussion of research along with any story they thought did not demonstrate an essential point. In a real sense they gave me no choice and I give you no choice, do exactly as you are instructed if you wish to become popular.

I was raised in Manhattan and my wife was raised in Johnstown, Pennsylvania, very different environments. After we were married we discovered we had one thing in common, the minute we didn't know the meaning of a word we looked it up. The reason we did this is we were both taught by nuns when we were very young and they insisted if you didn't know a word you immediately look it up. They claimed if you looked it up you would never forget the meaning. Even as a youngster I knew that wasn't exactly true but the nuns repeated that advice so often that we instinctively reach for a dictionary or a cell phone when we run across a word we do not know. If you hear any directive often enough in all probability you will follow it for most of your life. That is why, I repeat myself, insist that you reread sections of this text and memorize others. Becoming popular and remaining popular is a lifelong undertaking.

WORKING ALONE

Even though I know many readers would rather work alone I will repeat over and over that you're better off working with others and information that is reinforced by repetition is more likely to be acted upon. I will repeat how you must videotape yourself over and over particularly when you're looking for the everyday you. I will do this because it will increase the chances that you will ask your mate or a friend to help you when you need their help. Several times I will mention that you have to carefully study those videotapes. You have to look not only for negative looks on certain occasions but negative looks when you are listening to others. If you find yourself looking away when someone is speaking or rolling your eyes or smirking you must stop. Even very popular people occasionally make mistakes when listening to others, nobody is perfect. That is why everyone and I mean everyone must monitor their reaction to others on a regular basis.

Once again because I've given this course many times I know someone out there is saying I have a high IQ, graduated at the top my class from an Ivy League school and I do not have to reread sections or paragraphs to remember what's in them. That would be a valid argument if I were teaching you about popularity. I'm sure you would get straight A's on a popularity test but I'm not teaching you about popularity, I am training you to be popular. I'm not asking you just to reread those sections but if you get a chance reread them aloud in front of a mirror. Do this even if you almost memorize the material you are repeating because that will imprint them on your mind and increase the chances that you will act on my advice which will increase the chances you will become popular. So do it, do it, do it, it works!

I mentioned earlier almost everybody by copying those around them when they are children learn most of the signals they send as adults. The signals often change particularly for females when they enter puberty but that doesn't make much difference. If you're in your 20s or 30s and you wish to change these ingrained signals it's difficult, if you're in your 40s, 50s or 60s it's more difficult. Since the only way most of you can become popular is to change the messages sent by those signals learned as a child or young adult, you will fail unless you are willing to work very hard and do exactly as I suggest. So please, if you are not committed to working and following my instructions I ask you to put this book away until you are.

BEATEN BY LESS QUALIFIED PEOPLE

If you haven't gotten those promotions you deserve, 80% of the time it's because you are not as popular as those who have been promoted. Popular and unpopular people are seen from two different perspectives. If someone is liked by almost everyone when he or she makes mistakes they are seen as minor and forgotten by most while their accomplishments are not. However if they are unpopular their mistakes are seen as major and usually remembered. This text wil solve that problem.

BULLYING

If you're being bullied or doing the bullying it can destroy your life. This text will show those who are being bullied or engaged in bullying how to avoid that trap which can ruin your life. Work hard at learning to be popular because you are less likely to be a victim if you become popular and if you're doing the bullying you should understand the reason most teenagers bully others is because they are not sure of themselves and think by picking on someone else they will be more popular. It doesn't work that way the only way to become popular is to make others feel happy when they see you. This text will teach you, how to do that.

*   *   *   *   *   *   *   *   *   *   *   *

Join or start a popularity group today. It will dramatically increase your chances of becoming popular.

SECTION 1

BUILDING POPULARITY HABITS

This book is actually a sophisticated training manual. In 2 to 3 months it will train between 30% and 40% of those who follow my directions exactly to become popular and in 4 to 6 months it will train arround 80% to turn their charm on and off like a light bulb. It doesn't matter who you are, or how popular you are or have been in the past, it will work for you, period! In fact it works best for those who have been unpopular all that lives because they work at it.

"Molloy's Popularity Game" is also different because it's design was influenced by the same type of people who will read the book. For those who know my previous works they are filled with statistics and data. This book is not because the people who took my course said don't bore us with statistics just tell us what to do. So that is what I do.

The beginning of the book uses examples of behavior in business settings, because I spent most of my life consulting with businesses. However, the book is designed for everyone. The examples shown that demonstrate what makes one popular or unpopular are true for teenage high school students when dealing with classmates as well as for 50ish executives when dealing with the business world. The rules for being popular remain the same no matter who you are or where you are. So whether you are a businessman or woman, a teenager, a college student or a blue collar worker, if you work with this text it will work for you. That's the last time I'll speak of theory because my students were not interested in theory. They wanted me to deal with the real world and not waste their time.

This book is not designed to help you find out how popular you are, you already know. We all do. If you are among the one half of one percent who are popularity superstars, congratulations! I'm sure you are using your popularity to your advantage and you may not get much out of this book, though you should find it entertaining. If you are among the seven percent who are popular with most people but not superstars, you could easily become a superstar by following the advice in this book. If you are like most of us, who have a good number of friends but seldom receive preferential treatment from the world, or are one of those who have trouble making and keeping friends, or one of those who would rather text than talk, you *need* this book.

REREAD THE ABOVE PARAGRAPH

THE POPULAR LIFE

Popular men, women, and teenagers live in a different world from the rest of us. When we meet these charmers, we are instantly attracted to them and we are more likely to greet them with a smile and be friendlier to them than most others we meet. Life is pleasant for popular people, the world treats them better than the rest of us. When charmers speak at a social gathering, a business meeting or in class people including teachers are more likely to listen carefully and to find them impressive. Because they are so much fun to be around, they are often invited to socialize with the power elite in their companies and communities. They are more likely to be invited to parties, to join the teenage crowd going to the movies, asked to go on ski trips, or to go for weekends in the country, invited to a poker game with the boys, or to go shopping with the girls, become a member of the popular group in high school and to join the best country or yacht club in town.

Because being popular, opens both boardroom and bedroom doors, popular people are more successful both economically and romantically than the rest of us. Over four decades of working with the people who run corporate America convinced me that charmers were far more likely to succeed than Joe and Jane average, in large part because they are given preferential treatment. I also concluded that when those in power have to choose between a popular person and an equally qualified and sometimes less qualified but not quite as charming person for a promotion, a raise, a membership in a country club, an invitation to join the boys for golf or the girls for lunch, the vast majority will choose the popular person. Have no doubt; there is a positive correlation between being popular and being successful.

The popular are their own aristocracy, like the rich, the powerful, and the famous. Based on over twenty-five years of teaching people how to become more popular, this book will help you join their privileged ranks, dramatically boosting your chances of succeeding both socially and professionally. It will show you how to charm almost everyone you meet.

I expect most of you think that is impossible. We all developed our concept of popularity in junior high school, when raging hormones unleashed by puberty ruled, and those who were most attractive tended to be the most popular. That is why even to this day many 45 year olds believe either you have it or you don't but that is nonsense. Whether you are popular or not depends almost entirely on the signals you send and almost anyone can be taught to send the right signals.

I made my first discovery about how to train people to increase their popularity while teaching salespeople to sell. We knew buyers often made up their minds about a sale as a salesperson walked through the door, sometimes even before any words were spoken. When we analyzed their approaches and compared their sales we found that the salespeople who sent friendly, upbeat messages, through their body language, tone of voice, and overall demeanor, were more likely to make a sale. Once I made that discovery I trained salespeople to walk into the buyer's office looking more friendly and upbeat. It worked; their sales increased. Once word got out, companies started hiring me as a sales trainer.

I went on to teach my popularity and sales training course for over 35 years, and this experience taught me that at least 85% of people can easily be trained to send messages that will make them more popular. I've successfully trained everyone from a twelve-year-old girl who was having trouble in school, to two brothers in their seventies who were unpopular in their retirement community. I have in addition trained people who were unsure of themselves, and who considered themselves unattractive, inarticulate losers. I've also trained people who were socially inept and those whose disappointments in life made them antagonistic and caustic. Believe it or not I have trained people who thought the whole idea of being trained to become more popular was nonsense. My client companies sent salespeople and others to my course and told them to do exactly as I said. To their surprise and delight many of them became more popular, their sales increased and in most cases for the first time the people they met treated them like a friend.

Please note that in the paragraph above I used a version of the word train seven times. That was not an accident. This book is not designed to teach you about popularity; but to train you to be popular. It will succeed because the methods I employ are based on my extensive record of success.

SENDING THE RIGHT SIGNALS

Pretend that you attended a neighborhood party or a business meeting last night and met two strangers. The first was a very nice person easy-going, pleasant and fun to be around and the second you just didn't like; they appear to be bored by the party and by you or they seemed disingenuous, trying too hard to be charming. I am sure you've met plenty of both types. The first you might invite to a party you are giving and introduce to your friends or business associates. The second, you almost surely would avoid. Now think about how much you really know about each of them. Well, you know more than you probably think.

You react the way you do to these types because over the years, you have discovered that the people with whom you developed good relationships generally appeared friendly and easy-going from the start. You also found that those who seemed boring and untrustworthy often turned out to have reputations for being so. You are right most of the time, but not all the time. Some charming people turn out to be confidence men who are out to steal every penny you have, or at least up to no good.

Confidence men are invariably charming. They use that charm to convince people that they can trust them. On the flip side, some of those you don't like or trust, who you find boring or annoying, might actually be really nice, decent people you might like to have as a friend. But for the most part, you can trust your instincts; the process of evolution has provided us with a finely crafted tuning fork for judging people when we first meet them. This is why learning to send the right signals is so important and powerful.

The question is what are the right signals? I came up with a list of correct signals, which was no great achievement. If anyone studies popular people or great salespeople they will probably come up with the same or a similar list. My real contribution to the study of popularity is through trial and error, I developed a set of effective techniques for helping anyone change their unpopular negative signals to popular ones. 30 years ago I knew that a little over one fourth of us, without being aware we are doing so, regularly send negative visual and verbal signals. A significant percentage of people sending the signals turn off most of those they meet before they say a word. The negative messages men send most often announce that they are unfriendly, aggressive, or untrustworthy. Less popular women often announce they are either superior or inferior, both of which are off-putting, or signal, usually non-verbally, they are competing both socially and sexually with those they meet. Of course, the signals to which men and women respond either positively or negatively are different. Most signals that people respond to are not sent purposely but by accident or more accurately because they are a product of old ingrained habits. That of course is bad news, the good news is that those old ingrained bad habits can be transformed into good ones. To accomplish this I use indoctrination, conditioning, brainwashing along with a dozen other approaches but it all comes to the same thing, I change the long-standing ingrained habits that makes some of us unpopular into popular habits. While 80% of our students said our training worked Only one really knew how we did it. He was a former Marine Corps drill Sergeant who said he used the same techniques to turn American kids who were easy going and usually appalled by the idea of killing anyone into the best fighters in the world who reveled at the idea of killing the enemy. If he could turn kids into killers I'm sure I can using the same techniques turn most of you into charmers.

We found that learning to be popular is a physical activity, similar to learning to play golf or tennis. Golf and tennis players hire professionals to identify the flaws in their game and improve their performance by systematically correcting them. The same approach can be used when improving your performance in the popularity game. To quote one of my enthusiastic students, "Winning at golf and tennis is fun but wait until you start winning at life."

REREAD THE ABOVE PARAGRAPH

There is one major difference between learning to play golf or tennis and learning to be popular, no special talent is needed to become popular. If you hope to be a star golfer or tennis player you must be in fairly good physical condition and have above-average athletic ability. With popularity, just about anyone can become a star player. This is not true for young people in junior high and High School where popularity is measured by belonging to the right group. Cheerleaders and football players are most often popular while nerds and band members are not. That ends the minute you leave school, nobody cares after that. Once they become adults those popular kids are often butts of jokes. The only part of high school popularity that is important is how popular you are among your own group, if you're the most popular football player, cheerleader, nerd or band member you will be popular as an adult, if not, you won't.

Those who claim to be experts in the field of popularity almost always give the same advice: be upbeat, positive, friendly, smile, use people's names and become a good listener. Knowing this is not enough to make you popular. Developing habits that make those and other actions instinctive is the key. This book will teach you how to do that. What's more, you will begin to see results after weeks of implementing my advice and many of you will be astounded by how much better the world is treating you.

This will require just a bit of equipment. You'll need a simple videotaping device—a smartphone will suffice— at least one full-length mirror, several framed desk mirrors, a tripod, a TV, and whatever other equipment is needed to play the tapes you have recorded. These will allow you to discover the signals you are sending and to practice changing them.

REREAD THE ABOVE PARAGRAPH

Videotaping yourself is really the only way to discover the negative signals you are sending and when, where and under what circumstances you are sending them. That is why you must learn to discover the everyday you or more importantly each version of the everyday you. You must of course videotape yourself when you are interacting with others but you must also videotape yourself or have yourself videotaped when you're walking down the hallway, sitting at your desk at work and at home, eating lunch, sitting thinking, daydreaming, talking to someone you like and dislike, giving directions to subordinates, dealing with someone who's difficult, or doing any one of 100 things you normally do day in and day out. This is a very difficult task, it will take time, effort and the cooperation of others and then your work has just begun. You then have to examine those tapes very carefully with at least two or three people you trust. Tell them to pick out any picture they think sends a negative message. Then carefully look at that picture and say I will never put that look on my face again.

You must do this if you charm most people when you first meet them because of the 90% rule. If when you first meet strangers they think of you as enthusiastic, kind, friendly, self assured etc. and then they see you looking defeated, nasty, angry, sexually competitive etc. 90% will think that unattractive person is the real you. They will believe that when you appeared smiling, charming, engaging, and friendly it was an act. At that point they will not only dislike you they will despise you and see you as a phony who cannot be trusted.

MAKING NEW HABITS INTO INSTINCTS

The techniques I use in this text to train you are simple but they do require practice. They are designed to make your new positive habits instinctive. With instinctive behavior, you don't have to think about your actions. If someone asks you how much one plus one is, you immediately answer two without thinking. But if you're asked to add 86 and 37 or to name your cousin's three kids, you probably will have to think before responding. If you're asked to add 2612 and 9804, or to name Snow White's seven dwarfs or Jimmy Carter's vice president, you will probably need more time to think. The first type of answer is instinctive, the second is semi-instinctive and the third is calculated. I will train you in such a way that sending the right signals will become instinctive. That will require repetition. You must keep in mind that the object of this text is not to teach you about popularity but to make you more popular and in my classes I found that repetition of key points speeded up the learning curve.

Not only will I ask you to repeat information over and over I will be repeating it myself. For example, I explained how important good posture is to making a good first impression, nevertheless, a substantial number of students would show up for subsequent classes with the same poor posture they had when they started the first class. So I began repeating the message about posture. I will strategically repeat myself in this text for the same reason, it will help you to drill the changes you must make into your brain so that your new behavior becomes instinctive. I try not to make the repetition annoying but for most people that's impossible. My students said that although it was sometimes boring and dull they found it helpful and after a while they didn't object to such repetition because their lives had already begun to change for the better.

You can do a majority of the simple exercises by yourself, such as videotaping yourself while working at your desk at the office or at home which you can easily do with a smart phone. But you may also want to elicit the help of a spouse or close friend to give you feedback, or you may even want to form a group who will go through the book with you. A majority of my students have found that while most of the time they could work effectively alone, sometimes the input of others was very helpful. This was particularly true when they were identifying flaws in their message system and correcting them. I've found that those who worked alone were far less likely to correctly identify their flaws and when they did it usually took them quite a bit longer to correct them. That is why many of my students formed groups for practicing outside of class.

I strongly recommend when you start working on your popularity skills you get a friend to work with you. Then ask that friend to find someone who doesn't know you well to join the group and you in turn find someone who doesn't know your friend to join the group.

Teenagers often form groups of their friends, sometimes that works for them. If after you have formed one of those friends only groups and you find it isn't working, you must form or join a second group. Having four people working together will double your chances of succeeding. However, eight is the ideal number of members for a popularity group. Therefore when you are looking for a new member, try to find someone who doesn't know the others in the group. This takes time but it is well worth it. In addition, you should try to attract people from similar backgrounds because they will read each other's signals more accurately than outsiders. That does not mean you will not be popular with people outside your social circle because once you learn to be popular, it is a transferable skill.

REREAD THE ABOVE PARAGRAPH

The most common mistake made by people working by themselves is that they do not set up a schedule for practicing, which is one reason working in a group can be helpful. You may find a group at the office or at school who want to work together. In some offices that won't be too difficult because some managers believe if all their employees are involved in this training it increases their cooperation and productivity. However, proving that is impossible at this time. If you don't have a strict schedule and stick to it, you simply won't make as much progress as quickly as those who do. Some groups meet at a different location each week but I think it's best to meet in one place; that way you don't have to worry about bringing equipment from place to place. In my work with students, I've found that progress was quickest and surest if they limited themselves to no more than three meetings a week and no session ran more than two hours. But this is only a suggestion. Some individuals and groups I have worked with have spent considerably more time practicing and some considerably less. The real answer to how long or how much you should practice is whatever works for you.

Whatever you do, don't take shortcuts. Follow my instructions exactly. They are the product of many years of trial and error testing. For example, we discovered over time that those who practiced in front of a mirror rather than videotaping themselves had a harder time identifying mistakes in their nonverbal presentation because they edited their facial expressions and body language. When you are looking into a mirror, it's virtually impossible not to edit yourself. If you use a videotaping device, you may at first edit yourself but eventually you'll lapse into your normal behavior and the tape will capture that. Actually this works very well when practicing making a good first impression.

Most how-to books do not make these types of demands. I didn't run across one that asked the readers to monitor themselves so rigorously and insisted that they practice their recommended exercises for months. They promise you success the easy way. I'm not going to make you that false promise but I can tell you that you will see progress quickly and I am confident that your progress will inspire you to do the required practice.

Before diving in, I want to say just a bit more about popularity, so that the goal you're aiming for is totally clear.

WHAT SORT OF POPULAR DO YOU WANT TO BE?

Once I started formally researching popularity I had to come up with a definition. What popularity is might seem obvious but we found that it's not. I gathered seven of my best researchers, who had already been working for at least a year on discovering how to make salespeople more popular and I asked them to formulate a definition. They first assumed that being popular meant being liked, but they quickly corrected that. They realized that some people who are liked are not really popular. They have traded their dignity in order to associate with people who normally wouldn't accept them as friends or equals.

After interviewing members of these groups I believe they were often only accepted because they were the person to whom everyone else in the group could feel superior. When we questioned members of several groups, and asked if they could think of such a person, most said yes and those who said no usually hemmed, hawed and hesitated leading me to believe their answer should have been yes. I followed up by asking if they liked that person and almost all said yes. I believe they were being truthful. The interesting part is that when we asked the same people to identify their close friends, these groveling types seldom appeared on anyone's list, even when the group was very small. More importantly, when we asked those in high potential groups, such as members of very exclusive powerful business groups, members of influential country clubs, etc. whose members were expected to run companies or other organizations to name those in the group who would be in key positions in just a few years, the grovelers were hardly ever named. My researchers called this, "Doormat Popularity." This is not what you want to aspire to.

Our research identified a second type of likeable person you do not want to emulate. They are generally described as nice and pleasant but they are not often invited to join the power players for lunch or golf, etc. and those in power do not go out of their way to help these people. The comment made most about them when we asked why they weren't invited to do things was that they are okay but "just not my type." The researchers found on careful examination of the notes from these interviews that many of these people were popular only at first glance. Most of them made a good first impression, but generally failed to make a good second impression, and once people got to know them better, a majority avoided them. My researchers called this "Veneer Popularity."

When we dug into the responses further, we realized that many people had indicated that these people were obviously looking for contacts and weren't trusted. If a person is distrusted, even if he or she is good looking and at first glance very likeable, they are almost inevitably condemned to failure. Sure enough, we found that many of those we identified as this type were having trouble at work and often weren't popular with the opposite sex.

With these two groups in mind, we decided the best definition of popularity is "Being liked, respected and as a result being given preferential treatment."

YOU WANT TO BE INCLUSIVE AND PERSONALLY POPULAR

Two additional types of popularity are important; personal or situational and inclusive or exclusive. Those with personal popularity charm most of the people they meet in whatever arena; at social gatherings, at the office, even in chance encounters when out shopping or dining. Those with situational popularity are more successful at charming people in a particular arena; some of them are more popular at work than in their personal lives and for others it's the reverse. It's much more useful to be personally popular.

You also want to be inclusive in your popularity, not exclusive. Think back to high school and you will understand this distinction instantly. A majority of popular boys hung out with and talked to their friends more than with anyone else but they were friendly with almost everyone. While popular girls were almost invariably members of an exclusive group. I feel obliged to point out that this gender distinction is not a hard and fast rule, but for the most part, becoming inclusively popular is harder for women than men. A man can be a member of an exclusive old boys' club and continue to lunch two or three times a week with men who have no chance of joining. Popular businessmen generally interact in a friendly manner not only with men who are at their level but those above them, as well as those who are not as successful socially or in business. No matter what exclusive organization a man belongs to, he is free to associate with anyone he wishes. For women, social norms have dictated that they be more exclusive. As one woman put it, "It is not who you speak to but who you do not speak to that counts." But my research shows that while exclusive popularity may be more common among women everyone is more popular by being more inclusive. This book will teach you how to be personally popular in an inclusive way.

The first step is getting to know the, "Every Day You."

*   *   *   *   *   *   *   *   *   *   *   *

Join or start a popularity group today. Once it is formed arrange meetings with other popularity groups. The reason this is essential is your friends may not accurately assess your message system either because they don't want to embarrass you or they simply misread your signals. Strangers are more likely to accurately assess the messages you are sending. Once you know what you're doing you can correct your mistakes .

SECTION 2

THE EVERY DAY YOU

If you wish to become popular the first thing you have to do is discover the everyday you. How you appear to others when you are with individuals, with groups, by yourself, thinking, reading, working, watching television, walking along the street and so forth. You can work by yourself but you will learn more quickly if you work with others. If you do it by yourself you have to set up a camera or several cameras on tripods and videotape yourself for at least a week. These tapes will be most useful if you videotape yourself when you are interacting with others. The most effective way of getting pictures of you interacting with others is to have a third party make the tape using a cell phone. This makes it possible for them to tape you interacting with others without the other person being aware they are being taped. Of course it is easier if you have your spouse, a friend or a popularity partner tape you.

When you have at least 20 hours of videotape, examine them carefully and you will probably see how you look most of the time. Once again this is difficult to do on your own but it can be done. It will be very helpful if you get someone who knows you well to look at the videos and to pick out the ones that are the real you. Over half of you will find that there are several versions of the real you. That is not good, particularly if you are a woman. Popular people usually look more or less the same all the time. Sending different or mixed messages turns people off and convinces them that you are a phony. If your image says you are friendly 95% of the time while the remaining 5% says you are nasty, 90% of those who see both will believe the nasty one is the real you. So you will have to examine every part of those tapes even if you look nasty only occasionally, you cannot ignore it. If you wish to be popular you must replace even the occasionally unattractive you with a friendly you. One gentleman I worked with appeared to be friendly and charming most of the time but when he was alone he looked angry. It killed his career. A consistent message tells people you are the person you appear to be which is one of the secrets of popularity. So pick one look, test to see if it says you are friendly and stick with that look.

If you are working on your own you have to guess which is the likable you. However, it is very likely you will pick the wrong image. The only real option is to test. Get pictures of each version of you and have them shown to ten relative strangers who would be comfortable interacting with your friends. Ask them to score each picture on a 1 to 10 likability scale. If any picture gets 9 or 10 that is the likable you. If it gets a 7 or 8 you can use it but I wouldn't. Anything below that is a negative image and must be replaced with a positive or friendly one. I think even those who have the help of others must test the image they are going to adopt before working at making it their own. Once you discover the most likable you, take that picture and put it next to every mirror you own. Then practice that look every time you look into the mirror until it becomes the real you.

While videotaping yourself or having yourself videotaped is the main way to see the real you, there is another method that works for almost everybody and very well for some, it's called "STOP & GLANCE." Every time you approach a mirror freeze your facial muscles and look in the mirror. Many of you when you first try will see a surprised artificial you. That's not the look you're after. You want to see your face and body language as they are. You want to see the real you. Start by practicing looking into a mirror without changing the expression on your face and your body language. Look away and then look back in the mirror several dozen times. Don't try to look friendly, beautiful, charming, handsome but ordinary. It may take practice but eventually most of you will be able to do that. Next place mirrors around you and glance at each one as you go by. In just a few days you will see the you that everyone else sees, the real you, the everyday you. Once you have accomplished that you should STOP & GLANCE whenever you are around a mirror. This is not only one of the ways to see the real you it is one of the ways of discovering if the real you changes when you are with certain people, when you're performing certain activities, when you're resting, when you're thinking, when you're distracted, when you don't think you're doing anything and so forth. That is why as you read on you will see STOP & GLANCE repeated over and over. When you do glance in the mirror on your desk, this is a wonderful way of correcting reoccurring negative messages and probably the best way for many people who work alone to see themselves as the world sees them.

Why is that so important? Think about it, you make judgments all the time about people with whom you have never had a conversation. I bet you can think of at least three people with whom you have had only casual contact but who you are sure you would never want as a friend or coworker. Ninety-four percent of those we surveyed admitted they regularly made snap decisions about people, sometimes even before they met or talked.

Research shows that people make such judgments based on people's facial expressions, dress, body language, posture and diction to name just a few factors. They not only make judgments when they are interacting with a person but when they observe people without personal contact, when they are sitting at their desks, walking down a hallway, eating lunch, shopping, riding in an elevator, talking with friends and so forth. While a majority of people agreed that these judgments were based primarily on nonverbal signals, most had taken no steps to monitor themselves to see if they were sending negative signals. In our interviews, we found that even those who had some awareness of the messages they sent seldom understood how those messages affected the way people treated them.

IDENTIFYING YOUR MESSAGES

If you normally look friendly that dramatically increases your chances of becoming popular. All of us have a normal facial expression and normal body language. If you want to know what yours is simply have someone take pictures of you when you are not aware they are being taken. Show them to several close friends and have them pick out the picture or pictures they see in their minds when they shut their eyes. Next, have a friend show them to at least ten relative strangers whose backgrounds are similar to yours and ask them to judge you on a scale of 1 to 10. If you get 9 or 10, you are great, if you get all eights or above you might be okay but you should test again. Less than eight you have to work at your everyday look. I will repeat this advice because it is so important that you cannot ignore it if you wish to become popular or even likable.

Most of us have slightly different demeanor, speech patterns and body language, when we are out in the world, than we do at home. We also change our signals depending on the people with whom we are interacting, the circumstances under which we are meeting, as well as where and when we are meeting. Some are aware we are doing this, but most are not. I have been conducting research on a variety of subjects for decades which required my people to videotape subjects in a variety of settings and interview them on a variety of subjects after they were videotaped. I discovered early on that people changed depending on when and where the meeting takes place and that over half of those who made substantial changes in their signaling to suit a particular person or situation, did so without thinking.

People's limited awareness of the type of signals they are sending was obvious in cases where the subjects thought they were doing a good job of sending positive signals but actually weren't. Our videos showed, for example, that approximately 60% of those who consciously sent positive signals when meeting with a boss, or a potential employer, started off being respectful. They nonverbally said such things as, you're right, I agree, that's terrific and so on. However, within two to seven minutes some sent nonverbal messages of skepticism or rejection of what the boss or interviewer was saying; messages like, are you sure? or are you kidding? and so on. Most of us do not worry about the messages we send because only one in four realize that the everyday signals we unconsciously send often have a major long-term impact. Many act as if social and business skills are independent but they are not. If you wish to succeed, you must charm the people you deal with in business just as you would do in a social setting.

One reason so many of us are not aware of the negative impact of our signals is their importance varies depending on the nature of your relationship with those with whom you are dealing. There is an inverse correlation between the importance attached to signals you send and the closeness and length of the relationship of those with whom you are interacting. Your everyday signals tend to have a limited impact on what people with whom you associate every day think of you. They have already made up their minds about you. Those who know you best often come to almost totally ignore both negative and positive signals. When they are asked about some negative body language of yours they'll tend to say things like "Oh, that's just Al," or Sara just looks that way, she doesn't mean it" If you are someone who often looks angry or upset and they are asked about it, they'll explain that that's just the way you normally look. However, to those you deal with only occasionally and strangers, things are quite different. For them, you are who you appear to be.

STOP & GLANCE NOT ONLY NOW BUT WHENEVER YOU PASS A MIRROR

That is why you will never be popular unless you change your everyday angry look into an everyday friendly or at least neutral look. This is more difficult than it might seem. To begin with most of us have a half a dozen expressions we use through most of our lives. A majority of us copy those expressions from people we know or admire usually before our second birthday so they are well ingrained and difficult to change. In addition when you change your look, some of those who have known you for a while will think you are putting on an act and will respond badly. This has encouraged some people I've worked with to go back to being their old negative signaling selves, which is a mistake. If you persist and maintain your new more positive look, most of those who know you will come around eventually, some quickly, most in a few weeks or months. Some, however, will never change their opinion of you.

Unfortunately, approximately ten percent of the people who today are convinced you are angry, nasty, or untrustworthy will never see you otherwise. Since no one is ever going to be popular with everyone, I suggest you forget about them and focus on winning over the rest of the world. The good news is that getting everyone to like you is not necessary to being genuinely popular. Some people are just too far apart in experience and interests to ever really get along. The most popular person in a church sewing circle is not going to be a social star at a gathering of Hell's Angels. And the Hell's Angel who is liked by all his peers would find it very difficult to win over the ladies in that sewing circle.

I am not saying that you should try to change who you are. In fact, being proud of who you are, is one of the keys to popularity. Most of us like those who like themselves, Popeye expressed that feeling with his famous line, "I am what I am what I am." Liking yourself however is not enough, the critical factor is how you *appear* to others in your day to day interactions. Those who know how they normally look and sound are able to correct flaws in their verbal and visual presentation far more quickly and effectively than those who have no idea how they appear to others.

SPOTTING NEGATIVE SIGNALS

Most of us look as if we are concentrating when we are working. However, some people do not look industrious at work, even when they are working very hard. If you are one of those people and work for a boss who keeps up with exactly what you are doing, not appearing industrious when you are working will probably make little difference in his assessment of you. He will judge you by the quality of your work. However, if your boss does not work closely with you, he will tend to judge you at least in part by how you look at those few times he does see you working. Unbeknownst to you, he may form the opinion that you're slacking off which of course could kill your career.

STOP & GLANCE

Another common miscue is that a substantial percentage of people appear to be smirking or not serious or deferential enough when interacting with someone important in their lives e.g. a boss, a neighbor, a potential mate etc. This can have grave consequences for your business and social life.

Some negative signals are easy to uncover. Simply ask your friends and family if they have noticed you sending the nonverbal signals that might turn them off. While they may spot those signals because most people react similarly to the same nonverbal signals, there are signals that are not easily recognized by the general public. That is why you must take every opportunity to videotape yourself, ideally both at home and at work. If you can accumulate a half a dozen to a dozen tapes when you are interacting with people who are important in your social or business life that should be enough to allow you to spot your mistakes. Let me give you a few examples of people with whom I've worked to show you just how unaware we can be of our messaging and how harmful it can be.

NO INTERACTION NECESSARY

Charles took my popularity course even though he was planning to leave the company that was paying for the course. He worked for an insurance company as a fire underwriter at company headquarters in Boston. His department had two functions, administrative and consulting. When an underwriter in a field office had a question about a case, it was submitted to the home office, where it was handled by more experienced and skilled underwriters. Charles was one of those supervisory underwriters. He had been with the company twelve years and had an excellent underwriting record. But when the department head job opened up, he was passed over for someone less qualified. Charles was outraged and started looking for another position.

The reason he took my course was the same reason he was leaving the company. He had been a candidate for department head, and he thought he was going to get the job. He had seniority, excellent performance appraisals and had been acting as a supervisor of five field offices for more than three years, but he was passed over. When he asked why, to his surprise his supervisor admitted Charles was a better underwriter and a more experienced supervisor than the man who got the job. However, when word had gone around the office that Charles was going to become department head, several underwriters let it be known that they would likely leave the company if he were put in charge of the department. This was towards the end of the Clinton Administration when the economy was booming and companies were competing hard for qualified people, so their threat bore some real weight. The supervisor said he didn't know what Charles had done to elicit such reactions but he could not afford to lose the protesting employees. He had regrettably been forced to choose the other fellow.

Charles was shocked. He believed the eleven underwriters he worked with liked him. He gathered them together and asked, "Who said these terrible things about me?" They all claimed it was not them. "Well, someone did," he muttered in response. One of the secretaries then volunteered to find out who had blackballed Charles and why.

She came back after lunch with all the details. About a dozen underwriters whose desks were twenty-five to thirty-five feet from Charles's had an unobstructed view of his desk. They did not work for or with Charles but they would have been working for him if he had become department head. By watching him every day at his desk from that distance, they had come to the conclusion that he treated his people miserably. These people who had spoken against him were not those with whom he actually worked. Most of them had never even spoken to him, but they went to the supervisor and protested his promotion.

The secretary didn't say what it was that gave them their negative impression and he was surprised that he struck them that way. Charles wasn't Mr. Charm, but he wasn't by anyone's definition unfriendly and certainly not nasty. He decided that if careers at the company were made or broken on general impressions rather than performance, he didn't want to work there anymore.

Charles was incredulous that videotaping himself would do any good but when I pressed him, he did have someone in his department videotape him at work. The next week when we met, he told me, "I know what I'm doing wrong. I wrinkle my brow and narrow my eyes and look like I'm mad as hell when I'm on the telephone." Ninety percent of the time he was on the phone he was talking to an underwriter in a field office most of whom he liked. In fact, he couldn't remember ever being mad when he was on the phone and yet he could clearly see on the tape that he looked angry.

I told him that in order to stop sending that negative message he must replace it with a positive one. We tried various looks and decided that when he put his hand on his chin while he was on the phone, he looked thoughtful instead of angry. He then practiced this gesture in front of a mirror for about 10 minutes for several nights at home. After a few days, by checking how he looked in a small mirror he had placed on his desk at work, he could see he was making progress. At first he still regularly caught himself looking angry, but when he did, he immediately changed his expression. Soon a new Charles began appearing regularly in the mirror. After a month he had himself videotaped again and sure enough, the second tape showed a new friendly Charles appearing most of the time.

Making a change like this permanent requires vigilance; lifelong habits are hard to break. Because I had a long-term contract with the company where Charles worked, I requested that he report to me once a month. Even after three months of self-training, he still occasionally wrinkled his brow and looked angry. But after six months he very rarely did so. He had developed a new on-the-phone look and practiced so diligently that his new friendly image had become almost instinctive.

STOP & GLANCE

EVEN PRACTICED PRESENTERS MAY HAVE HIDDEN PROBLEMS

Three years later Harry a young TV reporter signed up for my popularity course. I assumed he wanted to take the course to be more popular with his audience, and I told him he was taking the wrong class, since my company had a special course designed to help news people, actors, executives and politicians be more popular on stage and on screen. I made my assumption because he came across as calm, confident, and articulate. But he dismissed my recommendation and insisted on staying in the popularity class. It was the next week before I found out why. Before the second class Harry took me aside and told me that on more than one occasion, those in management at his station had implied that they didn't think he was very bright. He figured his boss must have given them that impression, and he brought the issue up with him, but his supervisor assured him that he had never said anything to create that impression. Two months later, the news director took an assignment away from Harry and gave it to someone Harry didn't think was as well qualified as he. When he asked his supervisor why the news director had taken the story away from him, he told Harry he assumed that Harry had somehow offended the director.

Harry was good-looking, tall, and slim, with broad shoulders and a deep, mellifluous, authoritative voice. He had all the qualities necessary to become a network anchor. I could not see why anyone would get the impression he wasn't bright. Since Harry was on television, I asked to see a tape of him on the air, and if possible both before and after the show. He said that was no problem but he had reviewed his tapes and as far as he could see, he wasn't making any mistakes. The minute I looked at the videotapes he sent me I spotted his problem. Just before the show went on the air, Harry was sitting at his desk with his mouth hanging slightly open, looking inept. He had only looked at footage of his on-air performance, and his mouth hung open only before the show.

When I showed him the section of the tape from before the show, he exclaimed, "It's a family curse! My family has lung problems, my father had emphysema and my three sisters have asthma." He went on to explain that he found it a bit difficult to breath under the hot TV lights and I concluded that must be why he left his mouth open. But then we discovered a tape of him watching television in a room without TV lights and his mouth still hung open. Obviously, it was not the lights causing the problem. Holding his mouth slightly open was simply a bad habit he'd picked up and even though he was a professional communicator who was determined to break that unfortunate habit, doing so proved extremely difficult. Nonetheless, in two months, by first practicing in front of a mirror to make sure he kept his mouth closed, then practicing in front of a TV camera and examining the tapes afterwards and finally hiring a coach to work more intensively with him, he managed it. Someday I expect to turn on the network news and see Harry sitting there, with his mouth closed, looking like the next Tom Brokaw.

SOME BAD VISUAL HABITS ARE DEEPLY INGRAINED

Finally, let me tell you about Katie, who before the first class took me aside and asked if she could see me after class. When everyone had left, she played several short videos showing her hunching her shoulders forward in various situations. This made her look lower class. In each of the videos she was wearing a sweater, and when she sat with her shoulders hunched forward it came up to her neck. Although she was sitting behind a very nice desk she didn't look like she belonged. She explained that she developed breasts in the fifth grade, and when the boys stared at her bosom she became self-conscious and uncomfortable. Her solution was to wear loose-fitting tops and to roll her shoulders forward. "Unfortunately," she told me, "when men speak to me today, I round my shoulders and cross my arms in an attempt to cover my breasts. I just can't seem to break the habit."

I gave Katie the same advice I give to everyone with a similar problem, when you want to rid yourself of a bad habit replace it with a good one. In her case, the habit was the outward manifestation of deep-seated psychological scarring and she had to seek professional counseling in order to train herself not to do it. Remember that I have not promised you that changing your negative messaging will be easy. Sometimes it is fairly simple to do and at other times it takes long, hard work. But in either case, it's never going to happen until you identify the negative signals you're sending.

In most cases, if you videotape yourself over and over again under the same conditions, expressions and other nonverbal signals that are causing the problem will jump off the screen. This is highly motivating, once you spot your mistakes you will want to correct them. It's best if you think of doing so as an athletic challenge. When I trained students, I had them practice correcting their messaging mistakes as I watched. As they practiced I commented on their performance and corrected any mistakes they were making.

Of course I videotaped the sessions and when I played them back I realized I sounded like a sports coach, constantly urging them to:

Stand up straighter. No, no, that's too stiff. Relax your shoulders just a bit. That's better.

Walk across the room and sit in the chair without slouching. That's better. You've got it. Now walk back and forth three times sitting in the chair each time.

Walk a little quicker.

Walk a little slower.

You're using your hands too much.

You're holding your body too stiff when you talk.

You're invading that person's private space, lean back.

Smile a bit more. Not for just a second, keep it up.

Lower your voice. Slow down, speak more clearly.

Slow down your speech, remember you are speaking to men and they speak more slowly than women. Men like women judge the opposite sex by their own standards. If you speak too quickly they are less likely to take you seriously.

Looking directly at the speaker and nodding is a wonderful way of signaling that you are paying attention or agreeing with the speaker both of which are positive complementary messages. However, most men and just about all women nod too quickly and too much. The most effective way of signaling that you are hanging on to every word the speaker is saying is what we refer to as a minimal nod, while looking but not staring at the space between and slightly above the speaker's eyes. If at any time you begin to feel that the speaker is becoming upset or uncomfortable, stop staring immediately but continue to nod slowly with a serious but friendly or at least neutral look on your face.

The first chance you get, using first a mirror then a video camera roleplay that scenario several times. It's part of learning to actively listen.

REREAD THE ABOVE PAGE AND A HALF 2 or 3X, STARTING WITH OF COURSE

People have all sorts of quirks, they make unintended facial expressions, walk, talk and position their bodies, without realizing what they're doing or what type of message they are sending. I know when the average reader reads this statement they think I'm talking about someone else, but I'm not. Having taught popularity for many years, I know many of you are convinced that you know how you look to others. After all, you have been looking at yourself in the mirror every morning to shave or to put on make-up. But in fact, at least 60% of you do not see yourselves the way the world sees you. Your time in front of the mirror every morning has likely created an inaccurate view of the way you normally look. When most of us look in a mirror, we unconsciously stand a bit straighter and put a little smile or an upbeat look on our faces. The person that most of you see in the mirror is the person you would like to be. However, if you wish to learn to send the signals that will make you popular, you have to be able to see the real you, not a fictitious character you have invented so that you can feel good about yourself.

The simplest way to do this is to ask a friend, spouse or family member to videotape you when you are not aware of being taped. Tapes should be made of you doing as many things in your daily routine as possible: walking down a hallway, approaching the building where you work, driving your car, eating, watching television, and any other activity you perform regularly. Ask the camera person to zoom in on anything unusual or off-putting and to take regular close-ups of your face. It will probably take a few weeks to get enough footage, because in the beginning, you will be aware of being photographed, but as time goes by you will forget about the camera. At a minimum, you must be taped when you are walking, sitting, standing and carrying on conversations with a number of people who are or might be important in your life. If possible arrange to be videotaped with anyone who intimidates you.

These tapes will be most useful if you closely simulate your work and social environments. For example, if you work in front of a computer, set up a computer at home and sit at it and do some of your actual work. If you have a cushiony office chair at work, it's best to sit in a similar one for this exercise, and if you don't have one at home, I suggest you buy one or go to your office after hours and tape yourself there. The reason for this is that we have videotaped dozens of people who sat erect in a stiff-backed chair, but slouched when they sat in a padded office chair, and a majority of them changed their facial expressions when they were seated in different chairs. Sitting in the hard chair they looked alert, energetic, competent, and in charge, while in an office chair they often looked lethargic, inept, and bored.

REREAD THE 2 PARAGRAPHS ABOVE

DETAILS COUNT

Three young women who worked for a company at which I spoke on the positive effect of popularity training for executives and salespeople decided to use my techniques to improve their ability to sell themselves. One of the areas I covered was using videotaping to change the messages their executives and salespeople were sending to particular groups. The women decided to give the method I developed a try. Their objective was to figure out how they could improve their messaging to better attract men in a typical social setting. They started by videotaping each other acting as if they were at a party. But when they looked at the tapes, they could see that they carried themselves differently when being taped than they did normally. Their behavior was so artificial that they broke out laughing. For the second videotaping, they dressed the way they would when going out to a party, and carried on conversations with make-believe men. That did make their behavior more authentic, but they could still see they were acting for the camera. So they called me and asked what they could do to improve their tapes. I suggested that they role-play with people they knew.

They talked two of their brothers into helping them to make new tapes, which at first didn't work because their brothers immediately starting laughing and joking around when the taping began. The young women solved that problem by promising their brothers that they would teach them how to pick up women, if they took the taping seriously. They made three new videos, one on a Saturday morning, the second that Saturday evening just before leaving for a party, dressed in their party clothes, and the third on that Sunday afternoon. The change in their demeanor and overall body language in the Saturday night tape was striking. They looked more self-assured, upbeat, and sexy than in their other two tapes, and they realized that it was because they were dressed to go to a real party, with their hair styled and wearing high heels. This allowed them to see how they should change their messaging when they were meeting men.

I was impressed with the way they improved on my methods, revealing how details of dress and how they went about role playing dramatically impacted the quality of the tapes and their usefulness. From then on, I told people to re-create as closely as possible the real-life conditions they were simulating. After several tries we discovered the best way to do this was to pretend they were actually going to or at such an event.

REREAD THE ABOVE PARAGRAPH

TIPS FOR TAPING

If you have no one to tape you, place a video camera on a tripod and videotape yourself. For the first week or two do not even look at the tapes, they won't be useful because you'll be aware of the camera. But after a couple of weeks most people forget about the camera for at least ten to fifteen minutes several times a day. You will become involved in a project, a television program, or a conversation and forget you are being photographed. Once you realize that has taken place, look at the sections of tape shot when you completely forgot the camera was running. In most cases for the first time, you will see "the everyday you."

If you really cannot make a tape, you can ask a friend or spouse to photograph you when you are not aware it's being done. Here I am suggesting that you use the cameras in cell phones for this because that will give you instant results. I am repeating this because you must enlist someone who knows you well, to help identify the real you.

Ideally you should have someone who can close their eyes and see you. People who can do that are the best at picking out the real you. Ask that person to shut his or her eyes and imagine your face. Then look at the photographs and choose the one closest to the picture they had in their minds. Once that person has identified one or more pictures as the real you, you will have a pretty good idea of how you typically sit, stand, and move as well as the expressions and gestures you tend to make.

It is preferable to enlist someone who does not love you. Our experience shows that love really is blind; about one-third of those who love the subject did not spot flaws that pop out at others. If you can arrange to have more than one person go through the pictures, do so, but never have two people review the pictures together because the dominant person will influence the other.

I also advise that you use mirrors to get glimpses of the everyday you. Place one to the right and left of your television, across from you when you are eating, and at the end of a hallway you regularly walk down. After a period of getting used to the mirrors, if you glance into one of those mirrors you will be able to catch reflections of the real you now and again. Using mirrors this way will also be essential to monitoring your progress, so it is good to start using them early in your training.

STOP AND GLANCE

THEN REREAD THE ABOVE PARAGRAPH

As you go through your videotapes and photos, you will most often see one or two key looks or gestures repeated over and over that you realize are sending destructive messages. As I said before you will want to immediately eliminate them. This process may strike you as onerous, but I encourage you to give it a try. There is often a great side benefit for those who have themselves videotaped which our researchers called "the everyday you diet." Many of our students realized when partaking in this training that they had put on more pounds than they wanted. A number of them decided to lose weight immediately and they did. One gentleman started our class weighing 304 pounds and about year and a half later he sent me a picture of himself in a bathing suit at 196 pounds. At first I didn't recognize him but when I took a careful look I was amazed. While he represents an unusual case, weight loss was common among my students, I estimate 10% of the men and 30% of the women lost weight while taking my course.

Several times in this section I've told you to videotape yourself when you're interacting with people who are or who are going to be important in your life. If you do not have someone helping you that is a very difficult thing to do. Many of my students particularly those who worked alone set up cameras they could turn on with a button under their desk. Two of them actually bought cameras that were almost impossible to spot and set them up in their office or in their home. Do whatever you have to do to get those pictures.

ASSIGNMENT

Have yourself videotaped until you discover the everyday you.

*   *   *   *   *   *   *   *   *   *   *   *

Many businessmen are embarrassed to admit they are practicing to be popular. That's fine, you can do it on your own but it will take longer and be more difficult. However, you shouldn't be embarrassed because practicing to be popular will dramatically increase your chances of getting promotions and power.

SECTION 3

FIRST IMPRESSIONS

You should not underestimate the impact of the first two or three minutes when you meet someone, even though it is true that almost no one actually makes his or her mind up about a person that quickly. If you interrupt a first encounter after two or three minutes and ask people what they think of the person they have just met, most will give you an indefinite answer. They will say something like "He seems nice," "He is Joe's friend and Joe is a nice guy," or "I have no idea." They mean "I haven't figured him out yet." And because people are aware that they don't make up their minds about those they've just met that fast, they tend to underestimate the impact of those initial two or three minutes. The first impression we make may not seal the deal, but it often does have a major influence on what others think of us, how they will treat us in the future, and whether they will become our friends.

In fact, the first few minutes when you meet someone can be the most critical time in a relationship, even if it lasts for decades. I discovered this years before I started researching popularity. At the time, I was conducting a study of how image impacted an employee's chances of being promoted into management. As part of the study, I interviewed three men who worked as underwriters in a large insurance company. All three had been working for the company for twenty-four years and their qualifications and underwriting records were for all practical purposes identical. The first was a vice-president, the second a manager, while the third remained an underwriter. I questioned each separately about the other two. All three described the others as competent and hard-working. What caught my attention was that both the manager and the executive used the same phrase when describing the underwriter. Both said, "He turned out to be a lot smarter than I thought."

These two gentlemen remembered the day they met the third fellow. When he was being introduced, he was so nervous that he spilled coffee on his clothes, dropped the papers he was carrying and fumbled to pick them up. Their first impression was he was a klutz and not too bright. Two weeks later, he proved their initial impression incorrect by solving a complex problem. Nevertheless, twenty-four years later, when describing him, they referred back to their first impressions of him.

Over the years we interviewed dozens of people who described their long-term friends, coworkers, and even their mates, as smarter– or sometimes not as bright– friendlier, or more interesting than they thought. When we questioned them about when they had gotten that impression, they said they were referring back to their very first meeting. If you make a poor first impression, it may haunt you for as long as a relationship lasts, while if you make a good first impression, that will likely also stick.

STOP & GLANCE

A similar phenomenon takes place in real-estate-sales which real estate people refer to as curb appeal. Salespeople found that if prospective buyers were favorably impressed by the appearance of a house when they first caught sight of it, they were much more likely to buy. Twenty seven years ago my firm researched the impact of curb appeal for a real estate company. We walked thirty prospective buyers through a house. When we arrived with the first fifteen potential buyers, the outside of the house looked a bit shabby. The door was old and worn; the walkway was covered with leaves, and though the brick steps were sturdy, some of the grout was missing. Before the second fifteen prospective buyers arrived, we had a landscaper put in a few bushes and a handyman sweep the walk, paint the front door, and fix the steps. After each group saw the house, we asked them to tell us what they thought of the house, and then we asked about specific rooms.

When asked to describe the diminutive kitchen, the first fifteen said that it was too small, with thirteen saying they couldn't live with it. We also asked them to describe the living room, which was large for a house of that size. Only a few had anything nice to say about this large room with a pleasant view. When we asked the second group the same questions, they might as well have been talking about a different house. Seven of fifteen said they didn't like the kitchen, but they thought they might be able to live with it or said they could renovate it. Nine of fifteen said that they loved the living room. Their first impression from outside clearly had a major impact on their views of the inside.

A similar phenomenon takes place when people meet for the first time. If they are favorably impressed in the first two or three minutes, their further assessment will be colored by that favorable impression. They will tend to perceive your flaws as minor. Meanwhile, a poor first impression will generally lead them to see your flaws as major. Popularity superstars elicit strong positive responses from those they have known for only minutes. People who have just met them will often not only overlook but make excuses for negative signals they send. My research showed that more than ninety-six percent of them make a very good first impression, while the rest make a fair or neutral first impression. I only met one popularity superstar in twenty-seven years who created a poor first impression.

On the flip side, three to five percent of the population instantly turn off almost everyone they meet and approximately one in three of these people provoke intense dislike. The antagonism shown by normally reasonable, decent people towards them is astounding. When describing them, they often use expletives, such as "You wouldn't want to hire that SOB."

A majority of those who are instantly despised send one of two negative messages, or both. First, they convey that they believe they are superior beings because of their education, background or membership in some group. The other message they send is that they questioned the honesty, competence or credibility of the person they were meeting. Through the years in our research we encountered a number of these instantly unpopular people whose facial expressions and tone of voice announced that they do not give any credence to things being told to them. Usually without saying it aloud they're saying "I'll bet," "Yeah, sure," "You're kidding," or "Do you expect people to buy that?" I have seen people send this career killing message during interviews, and I heard cases in which people sent this message to their bosses and their clients.

Everyone when they finish reading the above paragraph says that's not me. The fact that you believe that is meaningless, it may be you, if only occasionally. The result of sending those messages is so devastating that you must check. Study every video tape you have for those signals.

A fellow who attended one of my training classes in Las Vegas was a classic case. There were only nine people in the class, but he was so annoying I had him sit aside so I could work with him after the session. When I explained to him that he had a constant condescending and questioning smirk on his face when talking to others in the class, he asked me to prove it. I played the videotape of him taken at the beginning of class when he was being introduced to his classmates. The minute he looked at it he was surprised and upset. For the first time in his life, he saw himself as others saw him. When he asked me to show him how to correct his problem, I knew he wouldn't be able to do it without practicing.

When the session ended, I told him I was going to take him to a cocktail party held by his company at the hotel next door on the strip. But first, I took him for a slow walk along the strip. While walking I had him practice greeting me with a smile and a friendly tone of voice over and over. At first, he had difficulty, so I told him to treat me as if I were someone he had admired all his life and had always wanted to meet. With that, his problem almost disappeared. I have been giving that advice for more than 20 years, and most of the time it works. It does not work immediately but after a dozen tries it usually solves the problem. With women it works almost instantly about half the time but very few women have this problem. However, whether you are male or female if you find that you have an almost constant smirk on your face that turns off most people, I suggest you give it a try right away.

When we arrived at the company cocktail party, I introduced him to the students who had attended the session with him about an hour and a half earlier. At first he was awkward, but after half a dozen introductions he was looking and sounding friendly and upbeat and he was changing their impression of him. I next had him spend an hour moving through a large meeting room in which the cocktail party was being held. He introduced himself as he moved from group to group. Everyone was wearing a name tag because the purpose of the gathering was for employees to meet their counterparts from other offices. I observed him closely, and later I informally interviewed nine of the people he had met. Six of them were willing to voice an opinion about him, and not one had a negative word to say. This demonstrates that even those with a serious problem can quickly and easily correct it.

NOT ALWAYS DECISIVE

The truth is, as important as a first impression can be, the assertion by many of those writing about the subject that a poor impression is permanent is nonsense. A majority of the articles I have read on first impressions contain some version of the old adage "You never get a second chance to make a first impression," which is a clever play on words, but is simply not true. Often we get several chances to make a first impression. If you meet someone for a few minutes and several weeks to several years go by before you see that person again, any impression you made has probably faded. So you get a second chance. Of course, there are exceptions. If you do something memorable, such as spill a bowl of soup in someone's lap or help a person out of a difficult situation, or if you meet someone at an important moment in his or her life, such as the first day on a new job, even if you have little or no interaction with the person again, the impression you made will be a lasting one.

Another reason first impressions are not decisive is that most of us on occasion make weak first impressions and some of us do it all the time. Weak first impressions tend to have little impact on most of those we meet. If Joe and Jane Average are introduced to fifteen people at a social gathering and spend five to ten minutes with each, a week later most of those they met will not remember their names. If their pictures are shown to those people, four to twelve will recognize them but a majority will not remember anything they said and will admit they have no idea what Joe or Jane are like. If they are asked the same questions right after the meetings, ten will give a thumbnail sketch of the strangers they have just met, often including an assessment of their characters. If they spend the next three to five days together and Joe and Jane do nothing to change the first impressions they made, those impressions will become semi-permanent. I say semi-permanent because if those people don't see Joe and Jane for several years, unless those five days were particularly memorable for some reason, when they meet again, Joe and Jane will in most cases start with a fresh slate.

The great myth about first impressions is when we meet a stranger we always make a first impression. Not so. Many create little or no impression. They neither charm nor offend. This can happen in business meetings even when it's the job of the people they're meeting to assess their character. When we asked business people what they thought of those who made weak first impressions, a typical response was "He didn't impress me," which of course has a negative connotation. Other comments were, "He didn't strike me one way or another," and "I couldn't figure him out." Most people who meet such "invisibles" do not remember their names or anything they said 45 minutes after they met. Those who make little or no first impression will most likely be forgotten almost instantly.

In business, making no impression is generally considered a sign of weakness. That said, if all you want to do is work at the job you're in until you retire, making no waves, according to some we spoke to, being invisible can be an asset. The managers we interviewed who expressed an opinion on the subject generally agreed that if you are "what's his name" in a large organization, while your chances of getting a promotion or a key assignment are dramatically reduced, your chances of being called on the carpet are also small, as well as the chance that you will be let go. In a social or social-business setting, making no impression is less problematic; it doesn't kill your chances of becoming popular with that crowd, but you'll have to create a good second impression which is unlikely because the same messages you need to send to create a good first impression are identical to the messages you must send to create a good second impression.

We'll discuss that more later, but first it's best to focus on making a good impression in the first place. Obviously, learning to make a good first impression will dramatically increase your chances of getting people to like you, to listen to you and to think of you as a friend and an honest and able person.

THE FIVE BEST WAYS TO MAKE A MEMORABLE FIRST IMPRESSION

The first requirement if you wish to be remembered is to greet people with enthusiasm, which you must calibrate carefully. If the meeting takes place in a business setting, you must curb your enthusiasm. Executives are often portrayed by Hollywood as stiff and dull and while that image is usually inaccurate and unfair, there's some truth in it. Most successful businesspeople have found that when they present a serious demeanor, they are taken seriously. At the same time being friendly and relaxed is also important. When we studied successful male executives we found that they were three times more likely to appear relaxed and friendly than their less successful counterparts. When we asked these executives in focus groups how they would describe their style and suggested a range of descriptions, the phrase most selected was "understated enthusiasm."

If you wish to be popular in any setting your enthusiasm should usually be understated. Do not grin like an idiot, shake hands with people as if you are exercising, raise your voice, or do anything else that comes across as over the top. To be effective, your enthusiasm must be warm, natural, and relaxing. Women have to pay very careful attention to this advice, they often overdo it. Many women in business smile too much or too broadly or are too enthusiastic. Studies have shown that women tend to smile more and more broadly when meeting people than men. That is expected and fine but the problem is that some smile too broadly, too often and at inappropriate times. If you think about the most popular women you know you will find that they smile only when it's appropriate. I've encountered some push back when I gave this advice. At a seminar for new employees at a client corporation, I advised the young women not to smile as much as they do. I said, if a young woman smiles all the time, the only thing they'll be put in charge of is getting coffee. I didn't mean it literally, but one young lady took umbrage, telling me that she graduated from Harvard and she didn't think she was going to be sent for coffee. I stupidly quipped that since she went to Harvard, she wouldn't be sent for just any coffee, she'd be sent to Starbucks. To put it mildly she was not amused. She said she was naturally a positive happy person and smiling was as natural to her as breathing and she was not going to change her personality to suit me. I knew I was not going to win that argument so I apologized and moved on.

When I returned to speak at the same company two years later she pulled me aside and said she wanted to thank me. At first she had ignored my advice and continued to smile all the time. But then a friend told her she heard one of the executives say that she was a nice person but wasn't ready for major responsibilities. The minute she heard that she stopped smiling as broadly or as often. Six months later she received one of three promotions given to those who started when she did and she thought the reasons were hard work, her Harvard degree and her new found serious image. This young lady worked in the marketing department and said that the minute she developed a serious image her ideas carried more weight at meetings which was important to her success now and in the future.

Many women, when trying to make a good first impression, gush and in most cases they don't realize they're turning off their coworkers and even some of those they meet in social settings. Some women give women a hug when they meet them. Never do that in business, particularly when men are present.

If you greet people with a full smile when you first meet, you'll be seen as friendly nevertheless, a pre-smile is better. A pre-smile is the look you have on your face when you're about to smile. In business barely smiling for only a second or two sends the most effective message a woman can send, it becomes even more effective if immediately after smiling she puts on a serious expression. But you must again carefully calibrate acting overly serious is a strong negative. That is one of the reasons it's best to work with a group because they will give you feedback.

You must also be careful not to give the impression with your enthusiasm that you're just putting on a show. Most of those who greet strangers with an upbeat, positive, friendly approach will be seen as people they would like to have as friends. However, if the minute you finish sending that wonderful message, you lose that friendly smile you will turn off the majority of those you have just met, people will see you as phony, or even dishonest. This doesn't mean you should keep a broad grin on your face, that would be overdoing it but you must continue to send the message that you are happy to have met that person.

The second thing you should do is to position yourself near the center of any group with whom you are interacting. People who make weak first impressions tend to hang back and stay away from the center of action, both in business and when socializing. In a business meeting you want to be engaged and heard by all. Office parties and similar social gatherings can be trickier, because people usually divide themselves into groups. Don't limit yourself to one group at an office party or at a social gathering. If you believe that it's likely you will interact in the future with those in attendance, it's your job to work the room. When you interact with a group, even for just a few moments, the people you have just met are more likely to think of you as one of them if you physically move into the group. In addition, it will enhance your chances of being seen as a member of the group if without seeming pushy you join in conversation with one or more members of the group. Once you've talked with anyone in a group, even for just a few minutes, those in the group are more likely to remember you and think well of you.

The third rule is to always dress with eye-catching style or flair. A simple way to do this is to wear or carry an unusual or attractive item, such as a well-tailored suit or a top-quality handbag. You should put your outfits together specifically with the intention of catching people's attention. Again, you must calibrate carefully. For men, in business especially looking too stylish can diminish their authority, while for women, being stylish is usually seen as a positive and will increase their visual impact without diminishing their authority. If you need help choosing the right garments seek out a clerk in a good clothing store they are pros and many of them will make good recommendations. However, if their advice strikes you as inappropriate follow your own instincts, remember most clerks are poorly educated and come from lower middle-class backgrounds which of course influences their choices.

We found that popular people also calibrate expertly how stylish they appear. They are usually only a little bit better dressed and groomed than most of the people with whom they associate which means almost never the best-dressed or the most stylish. While they put more effort into their appearance than seventy to eighty percent of their coworkers, they are careful not to be too chic, because they understand that fitting in is more important than looking good.

When we told women this, they told us we were crazy. They said every woman would like to be more stylish than her friends. But while women do generally pay more attention to their appearance than men, when our researchers compared popular and successful women to other women in their office, their dress was only a bit more stylish than most of their coworkers. When we showed videotapes of popular and average women to those women who first thought we were crazy, a majority admitted we had a point.

While conducting a totally unrelated study, we noticed that popular people were more likely to maintain their appearance throughout the day and almost four times as likely to go to the ladies or the men's room to check their appearance before they left for the day. Checking your appearance several times a day is necessary if you wish to dress with style.

The fourth step popular people often take when making a good first impression is they ask questions about the area of expertise of the person they are meeting. Then listen with riveted attention to what is said. The most common way of sending a negative message is to glance around when someone is speaking to you, that sends the clear message to most people that you're not interested in them or what they are saying. Too many of us do this all the time.

And the fifth commonly used approach by popular people is they ask those they have just met to do them a small favor, such as to hold their drink for a moment or to move over a bit on a couch so they can sit down.

Let us review the five techniques for making a good first impression:

1) Understated enthusiasm

2) Positioning yourself in the center of any group

3) Dress with eye-catching style

4) Ask friendly questions

5) Ask for small favors

MEMORIZE THE ABOVE FIVE

THE FIVE STEPS NEEDED FOR SALESPEOPLE TO MAKE A GOOD FIRST IMPRESSION

In our research with salespeople, we discovered that there are five distinct steps at a first meeting that increases a salesperson's chances of making a good first impression. While not identical there are similar steps that will increase your chances of making a good first impression in most social settings. It's important to be aware of these so that you can master them.

Recall that we placed cameras in buyers' offices and arranged to have salespeople from client companies videotaped when they made sales calls. We then played these videos for the buyers and asked them why they bought from one salesperson and not another. Even when they knew the reason they turned down a salesperson, when they were asked exactly what the salesman said or did that turned them off, most could only guess. Our solution was to put a switch under the buyers' desks and ask them to push it one way when they received a positive message and the other when they received a negative one. Recording the movement of the switch on the videotape let the buyers see exactly when they reacted to a positive or a negative message. This often enabled them to identify exactly what the salesperson did or said and how it affected their decision.

We also tested salespeople approaching buyers at country clubs, over lunch or dinner, on and off the golf course and dozens of other locations. No matter where, when or under what circumstances we tested how salespeople made a good impression on the buyer in most cases their approach could be divided into five parts.

The first is visual impact which is created when the person walks into the buyer's sight.

The second is the introduction, when the salesperson shakes hands with the buyer and says hello.

The third we call settling in.

The fourth is how they start a conversation.

And the fifth, is the ending, when the salesperson says good bye and leaves.

VISUAL IMPACT

To my surprise, most buyers pushed their switches before the salesperson said a word. They usually pushed it before the salesperson reached their desks. What was even more surprising was that their reaction to the salesperson as they walked in the door was the best predictor of whether or not they would buy. We found the same timing took place in singles hangouts. When we told young people this they said they were not surprised, good-looking guys and girls were winners when they walked through the door. However, we did take that into consideration. We attempted to level the playing field by taking the same young men and women and changing their approach. Only then did we question the people they were approaching. The vast majority made up their minds about the person before that person spoke. Making the impact stage the most critical element of a first impression.

This is interesting because when we tested people's reactions in social and traditional business settings they were virtually identical to those in sales situations. One significant difference is that the impact stage, which is largely nonverbal, and the introduction, which is both verbal and nonverbal, usually take place simultaneously in most social and traditional business settings.

In sales, social and traditional business meetings, when people have as little as three minutes to size you up, they will. Like buyers, they immediately make critical decisions about you that probably will affect your future relationship. The first thing they decide is whether you are the type of person with whom they would like to associate. We conducted these experiments for more than twenty years, partially as research but mainly as a teaching tool. After just a few sessions we realized that in both social, traditional business and sales situations there are several approaches that will help you make a good first impression.

When you first come into another person's presence, you should try to catch that person's attention and acknowledge them with a subtle smile or slight movement of your head. Remember, when people receive the message that you are paying attention to them, they are more likely to respond positively to you. You must look friendly but most of all interested in the person you are about to meet.

Obviously, it would be inappropriate to walk into a funeral or a serious business meeting with a smile on your face. Whether smiling is appropriate or not is a judgment call. If the meeting is by its nature serious, you are more likely to receive a positive response if you show respect for the person you are meeting by non-verbally acknowledging his or her presence with a small smile or a simple nod of your head.

What you must not do is look angry, aggressive, unfriendly, or dull, which a surprising number of people often do when they first meet someone. When we told students in our classes that they looked angry and aggressive, unfriendly or dull the majority of them didn't believe us. The most common reaction was to ask if they could try again. They were convinced our judgment was mistaken. If they did send negative messages, it was an accident they would not repeat. It wasn't and most of them did repeat the mistakes over and over. Our answer was the tapes. Once they looked at the tapes and saw the way they greeted the other students you would expect them to be convinced that the mistakes were theirs but they were not. A majority responded with disbelief followed quickly by denial and usually accompanied with an angry look. This occurred even when they were told by members of a popularity group they had joined because they wanted someone to look at them and tell them what they were doing wrong. The exercises I suggest at the end of the chapter will help you discover whether you're making any of these mistakes and outline the steps you can take to correct them.

The look that you want to strive for is a look that says to people, "I like and respect myself and I like and respect you." One of the great secrets of getting people to like you is convincing them that everyone likes you. When Joe and Jane Average meet someone they invariably send the message "I hope you like me." Joe and Jane popular, by contrast, send the message,

"Of course you are going to like me." When we looked at videotapes of popular people we consistently found they sent the message that they liked and respected themselves.

REREAD THESE 5 STEPS 2X or more

THE 5 STAGES OF A GOOD FIRST IMPRESSION

1) INITIAL CONTACT

We asked popular people how they acted when they met others. Most could not answer that question, so we made videotapes of them greeting strangers. After watching these videos a majority conceded their facial expression could be looked upon as an almost smile. When we asked what followed, almost all of them said they put out their hand and said pleased to meet you or its equivalent. Both popular men and women agreed; some, only after watching videos of themselves greeting people a dozen times or more. Most popular people moved closer when they shook hands and made eye contact with the person they were meeting. Twenty-two percent of the popular people we interviewed added without our asking that they shook hands without hesitation.

2) SETTLING IN.

There is a point in every introduction when both parties should pause. In most sales presentations, this occurs when the salesperson sits and settles in a chair. In social-business exchanges most pause after they shake hands. This little pause allows both parties to become comfortable. You always want to relax those you have just met and one way of doing this is to give them a chance to catch their breath. If you do not pause, many of those with whom you are interacting will react negatively. This is why popular speakers usually pause before they speak. They are sending the nonverbal message that they are relaxed and easygoing, which makes them non-threatening and likable. In our class videos, when students started speaking before the person they had just met had a chance to settle in, the body language of those to whom they were talking often became defensive and a few became antagonistic.

There are two additional reasons to wait a second or two before you speak. First, most popular people lean in a little when shaking hands, which is seen as a friendly gesture and often helps create a good first impression. But when you lean in you invade the other person's personal space and pausing before speaking lessens the sense of invasion. The second reason is that it creates the impression that you are confident because you appear calm and that sends the message that you are self-assured.

3) REMAIN CALM

Interestingly, the vast majority of those we tested reported that people who appeared calm were also more attractive. Not surprisingly when single men and women met they were more attracted to those who appeared calm. So if you are in a singles environment one of the best things to do, whether you are a male or female, is to slow down your speech and approach. This is particularly true for men because if they look nervous it turns off most women.

When we instructed salespeople to take a breath before they started their presentations, it increased the percentage of buyers who liked them. It also increased their sales particularly when they were selling to women. The same buyers said they liked the sales people we trained because they seemed friendly and self-assured. In business meetings the same actions had the same effect. After you have shaken hands and said hello, take a deep breath before you speak.

4) CONVERSATION

When making a sales presentation, the salesperson must initiate the conversation. He cannot wait until the buyer speaks. If he does, a substantial percentage of buyers will become annoyed. In business, time is money, and they will think that the salesperson is wasting their time. Salespeople must begin to speak as soon as they settle in while in a social situation it is preferable for the other party to speak first. Popularity superstars in both business and social situations encourage the other person to speak by asking questions. It is a wonderful way to start a conversation.

Since a first impression usually takes between two and three minutes, the conversation is of course limited. You will be judged not so much by what you say but how you say it. Most successful and popular people sound like the rest of us and exchange pleasantries when they first meet someone. If you break with convention and say something outrageous or confrontational you will annoy others, making it almost impossible to create a good first impression. Even those who are outrageous, unpleasant or confrontational by nature usually avoid being so when they are first introduced.

If your voice reminds people of chalk on a blackboard it can kill your business and social life. A classic example is Janice on Friends, who opens most conversations with "Oh my God" in a screechy, high-pitched, nasal Brooklyn accent. She, of course, is the character nobody likes. The problem isn't that these people sound terrible, because that can be easily fixed. The real problem is that they don't realize how they sound. A substantial percentage of them believe they sound like everyone else. So unless you are sure that you have a mellifluous voice, I suggest you have a conversation with the tape recorder and ask a friend to play it for at least five people who do not know you. If even one is annoyed by your voice, you must contact a speech coach immediately. Do not go to a voice coach. While some of them are excellent, others are incompetent. The safest bet is to contact an instructor in the speech department of your local university. They are invariably competent and usually excellent. They will analyze your speech and make suggestions for improvement. Don't expect wonders. You cannot expect significant improvement after one or two visits. It takes at least several sessions to get rid of a chalk on a blackboard sound.

The good news here is that approximately only 1 in 170 has a voice that stops them from getting along with others. They are such a small group that it was almost impossible to get an accurate number.

5) ENDING A FIRST MEETING

Since a first impression usually takes only a few minutes, you may wonder why I am spending time telling you how to end a first impression. The reason is simple. Often at a social or business gathering you will be introduced to a number of people and spend just a few minutes with each. The very nature of the event requires that you move on to meet others almost immediately. It is important to leave gracefully, maintaining an upbeat, positive, friendly, relaxed persona. One of the best ways to maintain a positive image is to pause for just a second before leaving. If you are sitting, stand for a couple of seconds and let your clothing fall out before you move. You will look better. it's a model's trick.

REREAD THE FIVE STEPS 2X

About one-third of our students made the mistake of thinking that the minute they start to leave they can stop sending upbeat, positive messages. Nothing could be further from the truth. A poor exit will often destroy an excellent first impression. When the people we were training stopped smiling, started slouching, and worst of all turned their backs on people who were still speaking, we could clearly see the negative reaction of those to whom they'd been talking. It showed in their faces and body language and it came up in the post-meeting interviews.

WATCH WAITERS AND WAITRESSES

A great way to see the stages of making a good first impression is to watch a top-notch waiter. In fact, I suggest everyone, no matter how good you think you are at making a good first impression, spend time watching how the best and most successful waiters and waitresses approach customers. Of course, some servers are better at this than others and some are absolutely terrible. You will spot the talented ones right away. They tend to make more than their co-workers because patrons tip them generously. Part of the reason is that they get orders right, anticipate customer's needs and deliver meals in a timely manner. But their secret is that they become their customer's friends. Often, patrons are so impressed that they request to sit at one of the server's tables whenever they come in to the restaurants where they work.

When watching waiters and waitresses don't stare that will make them nervous and you will come across as creepy. You must observe surreptitiously. I know that seems like a lot of trouble but it's worthwhile. Some of my very best students, those who I thought had nothing more to learn, told me that when they watched waiters and waitresses they noticed they send very subtle signals that charmed their customers. These talented students admitted that this never would have occurred to them. Even more importantly students who were having problems sending signals that would make them more popular after watching waiters seemed to catch on.

Believe me it's a worthwhile undertaking and from what my students tell me a lot of fun.

I would love to tell you that watching servers was my brainchild but it was not. A real estate saleswoman who took my popularity class gave me the idea. She told me about taking a couple to lunch to close a sale. She realized after five minutes that she was not going to sell that house or any house to them. The couple's questions were almost insulting. Without ever saying so, they questioned her honesty and everything she said about the house and the neighborhood. So she decided to sit back and simply try to enjoy lunch. Since she was paying for the meal, she thought the couple had a great deal of nerve to tell her she should leave a generous tip because the waitress was so nice. She usually tipped fifteen percent but she left an extra couple of dollars because, in fact, the waitress was the only part of the meal she had enjoyed. It was after she left the restaurant and the couple drove off that the thought occurred to her. She had spent almost three hours with that couple, trying to gain their confidence and in just a few minutes a waitress had charmed them. At first she was annoyed and then she decided to figure out how the waitress did it. She had lunch at that restaurant a minimum of three times a week for five or six weeks. Each time she observed how that waitress approached customers and reported her findings to me.

At the end of the fifth week I had lunch with her at that restaurant. The waitress, who was not a beautiful young woman, as you might have thought, charmed everyone, including me. I went back to that restaurant dozens of times, in spite of the fact I didn't care for the food, to find out how she did it.

I gained so much information from watching her that I decided to conduct a study. I identified a half a dozen restaurants where one waiter or waitress always charmed the customers and I ate at those restaurants repeatedly. In addition, I enlisted more than two dozen people who ate out all the time and asked if they had a favorite waiter or waitress. Almost all of them had one and 15% named two or three waiters they thought were terrific. I had them describe their server and tell me what they knew about him or her. One of the characteristics of all charming waiters is they treat their customers like friends and I know this is because these customers knew details of their servers lives. What surprised me even more was these popular waiters knew more about the customers lives than I thought they would.

As soon as we started interviewing waiters many of them told us they were not the top producers in their restaurant, nevertheless, we interviewed them. While we were doing these interviews I realized that the information we were getting was very valuable. Their answers clearly defined the difference between a good waiter who was liked by most of his customers and a popular waiter who charmed almost everyone. I also observed the top producers were almost invariably charming and personally popular.

Popular, charming waiters worked in every type of eatery from four-star restaurants to greasy spoons although a majority worked in chains that cater to the general public. At first glance you would think they had little in common, for example one of the techniques used by many very popular waiters is to squat down next to the table and put themselves at or below eye level with their customers while waiters in four-star restaurants almost never did that. This trick is often used by tall waiters and waitresses in moderate priced eateries. They use this technique because life has taught them that if they lean over people they intimidate them and turn them off. Charming waiters in four-star eateries achieve the same effect by leaning and or standing back from the table.

Good waiters look upon the table as the personal space of the diners and they do not enter that space without permission. When they pick up menus they don't ask for permission but if you watch them carefully they send nonverbal signals that clearly tell diners that's what they're about to do. Obviously at this point the diners could object and if they do the popular waiters will not pick up menus. Before they do these charmers usually get the nonverbal approval of the diners.

Not invading another's personal space is one of the primary characteristics of popular people. This is not how they act when they are dealing with friends however, it is almost a rule when they are interacting with those with whom they have a friendly relationship. The way waiters treat the diners table is similar to how popular and successful salespeople treat a buyer's desk. Without getting permission successful sales people almost never put anything on a buyer's desk. While women object to anyone invading their space particularly a male they are the ones who most often offend males by invading their personal space. If you are a woman and the man you are talking to starts very subtly and slowly moving away from you, back off, you have invaded his personal space. That makes him uncomfortable and that is why he is moving away. Once again before invading anyone's space ask for permission or at least announce nonverbally that that's what you're about to do. Don't do it without good reason and move out of the other person's personal space as quickly and as smoothly as possible. You can learn to do that by watching popular waiters.

Speaking of smooth movements popular waiters hardly ever hesitate either verbally or physically. We found when salespeople walked into a buyer's office without hesitating buyers generally liked and trusted them. Of course they introduce themselves and then after a very short pause start to speak which helps them reinforce the positive message they just sent. Popular waiters approach their customers in a similar fashion, like all popular people they introduce themselves and take a breath before speaking. When they tell the customers about the daily specials they either have them memorized or read them and of course they don't hesitate, they don't fumble or mumble but speak clearly and calmly. Popular waiters like most popular people appear calm, cool and collected.

If you have any nervous habits you must eliminate them. One of the best ways to do that is to replace them with calm, cool and smooth movements that give the appearance of someone who is unhurried and unworried. Popular waiters are often wonderful role models because while working swiftly they hardly ever look like they are hurrying.

Finally and most importantly, popular waiters always look pleasant. That doesn't mean that they are smiling in fact when popular male waiters approach customers for the first time 80% to 90% have a neutral look on their faces. Popular waitresses often have a small smile or a pre-smile. That works for women who are expected to smile more than men. However, not all popular women smile many have a neutral but pleasant look on their faces when they first meet someone. Believe it or not a pleasant neutral look is the most difficult facial expression to master and since finding a few facial expressions that you think would work for you watching waiters and waitresses can be very helpful. You have to carefully study their faces but you can't let them know you are doing it or they will become self-conscious and probably change their expression. There are two methods that work well: first the cross over techniques used by sophisticated researchers when observing people. They start by looking three or four inches to the right or left of the person they are studying. It will seem to the person being studied as if they are looking at someone or something behind them and few are ever upset by this. Then they carefully cross the person's face pausing on it for only a second and then moving on. The second and by far the best method requires the use of a smart phone and the assistance of a second party. Choose the person you wish to imitate and have your friend or your significant other stand or sit in front of them. Then take either a video or a simple picture of your assistant with the server you wish to emulate in the background . You can also take a selfie with the waiter you wish to copy in the background. I think a video works best. I suggest you take more than one picture. It's best if you pick someone who looks a bit like you but that is not required. It is necessary to pick someone of your own gender.

Through trial and error we found that using a mirror and pictures of someone you wish to copy is the easiest way to change your look. Don't try with the expression you think makes you look pleasant, instead try several expressions that you and others think make you look friendly. We found that often, the pictures that people choose for themselves are not the right ones. That is another reason joining a popularity group is very helpful. When you're attempting to imitate a friendly upbeat expression have several friends or others standing by and commenting. You may end up with an entirely different look than you would choose but it will be one that others respond to positively. Once you've chosen a friendly look, practice, practice and practice until that look is as natural to you as breathing.

STOP & GLANCE

POSTURE

Another thing you must do in order to make a good first impression is to appear erect and relaxed. Our testing shows that one of the best ways to send the message that you are self-assured is to pay careful attention to your posture. Fortunately, improving your posture is a relatively simple task. One method is to get three washcloths and roll them up. Then after bracing yourself against a wall place one on your head and one on each shoulder and walk around until you can keep them in place without great effort. Once you have mastered that, try to keep them in place while you go about your normal activities (probably best to do this only at home.) A number of women claimed that using the old English finishing school method of placing a book on their heads and practicing balancing it while walking and sitting down and getting up worked for them. They have a point because most women carry their bodies in an erect manner, the main difference between the upper class and middle class women generally is the angle at which they hold their heads. Try either method while going about your normal activities. Before you attempt this exercise, make sure you are well away from breakable and valuable items; a falling book can do a good deal of damage.

Because the way we carry our bodies is a strongly ingrained habit, you will have to do these exercises once a week for several months to make your new image instinctive. In the beginning you will probably walk stiffly, like a West Point cadet. If you find yourself doing that, you'll have to work at relaxing your body while remaining erect. Of course, having a ramrod straight posture can sometimes be effective in business; it can make you look authoritative or even intimidating, which is a skill you may find useful if most of the time when you are erect you look self-assured, friendly, non-intimidating, and non-judgmental. The thing that makes this exercise difficult is a majority of you when you attempt to appear relaxed and yet erect is the minute you stand erect you automatically stiffen your body, A reoccurring problem that arises for some women and many men is once they become erect they change the expression on their faces. Their expression goes from being friendly, relaxed and easygoing to authoritative and often judgmental. That is why you will continue to see the words STOP & GLANCE often where you least expect it. When you do, without changing the expression on your face, look in a mirror and see if while remaining erect you still look friendly and approachable. If you don't, you have to work at correcting that immediately.

First in front of a mirror and then for a video camera, practice greeting a stranger in a friendly, smooth, casual, relaxed, unhesitating manner.

Second, while walking toward a mirror, and then toward a video camera, practice acknowledging the person you are about to meet with eye contact, a small smile, or slight movement of your head.

Third. in front of a mirror, and then a video camera, practice greeting people like old friends.

Fourth, improve your posture by balancing a book if you are a female or three rolled-up washcloths if you are a male or female. Do it first when walking, then sitting, and after you have mastered that, as you carry on your everyday activities. It helps if you practice before a mirror. Repeat these exercises in front of a mirror at least half a dozen times a day for a week before moving on to videotaping. Then, keep videotaping yourself until seven consecutive tapes show you greeting everyone with enthusiasm, and as if they are old friends.

REREAD AT LEAST 5X

You should also elicit the help of a friend or your spouse to act as a monitor of how you are greeting people as you go about your everyday life. If you are being monitored by people who know you well, they may overlook your flaws. They will be far more effective if they are instructed to watch you very carefully and look for flaws. If you are working with a popularity group, you should be monitored by as many members of the group as possible. When you attend a business or social function, only one member of your group should be assigned to monitor you. The one thing you do not want is that person's analysis to be affected by others. Do not get upset if the reports contradict each other. People see the world differently and they may see you differently. It is only after reading several reports that you will begin to see recurring flaws and suggestions for remedying them. When this procedure is followed, most of you will be able to identify and correct most of your damaging nonverbal signals.

VIDEOTAPING

As with the exercises in section 2, you should also arrange to have someone videotape you when you are actually meeting people for the first time. This is difficult, especially in a business setting because the people who run business gatherings will probably object to your videotaping. People at social functions are as likely to object to your videotaping people at their parties. However, with cell phones people can discreetly make videos just about anywhere without others noticing.

PRACTICING

After discovering your mistakes and coming up with an effective way to overcome them, the real work begins. If you have been greeting people without enthusiasm for years, you will probably greet everyone you meet for the next week with enthusiasm. However, we all are creatures of habit and as time goes by you will find yourself once again greeting people like your old dull self. When an old ingrained habit resurfaces and many of them will, you must change it. We found the best way to change old habits is to replace them with new ones. For example teach yourself to be instinctively enthusiastic, by repeatedly walking up to a mirror and then a video camera and greeting a person with enthusiasm. Once you have appeared enthusiastic three or four times in front of the mirror and a video camera you should repeat the exercise as many times as necessary until it becomes instinctive. Even after you have succeeded you have to check back on a regular basis to avoid falling back into old habits. It will bore you but you must continue to practice until you think about being enthusiastic whenever you greet someone.

After practicing the same exercise until it becomes boring you will find that just before you greet someone you will think about being enthusiastic and that will affect how you act, There are times when your enthusiasm will be instinctive but there will be others when it will not, keep at it until it is almost always instinctive.

Keep practicing until being enthusiastic becomes as natural as breathing.

REREAD AT LEAST 3X

* * * * * * * * * * * *

There are a number of ways to arrange for meetings with other clubs; Popularty Groups on Facebook, personal contacts, Facebook and Twitter are the most effective.

SECTION 4

SECOND IMPRESSIONS

This section deals with the messages you send after you've made a first impression and before strangers decide if they know you well enough to make a final judgment about the type of person you are. This second impression is the heart of popularity and for most it's a make-it-or-break-it time.

THE STAYING POWER OF A GOOD SECOND IMPRESSION

Second impressions can and often do last a lifetime. Consider the impact of a good second impression on one young woman's career. She was from a small town in South Carolina and had just been hired as an attorney by a major New York law firm in the early 1990s. She is now a partner. One of the reasons she has done so well is that she quickly developed a reputation for being feisty. On her first day, she was introduced to two young women attorneys, who had been working at the firm for a year. She was nervous when she was introduced and suspected she hadn't made a good first impression, but they invited her to lunch. She felt out of place at the restaurant because it was fancier than anything at home and she wasn't as fashionably dressed as the other two. When the fish she ordered was placed in front of her, she discovered right away that it was dried out and it looked as though it had been reheated. She asked the waitress to have the kitchen prepare another meal but the server pretended not to hear her, turned her back and walked away. The young woman stood up and yelled after her, "Get back here and take this dried-up garbage to the kitchen," which made a powerful second impression on her lunch mates. What's more the manager came right over and her meal was replaced. Her reputation as feisty was established.

When I asked why she became so angry, she explained that when the waitress had clearly decided she didn't deserve first-class treatment, she had been intimidated and she was ashamed of being intimidated. Since she had arrived in New York, she had been feeling that way and it made her angry, mainly at herself. When the waitress turned her back on her she reached her boiling point. The irony was, back home, she was known as the quiet girl in the back of the class. But even after she told her new friends that, they continued to think of her as a fighter and the word that she was spread throughout the firm.

LASTING IMPRESSIONS ABOUT THE MASS MURDERER NEXT DOOR

Research shows more than sixty five percent of the time, the long-term impressions people form are almost identical to the second impressions they formed earlier. Just think about the kinds of things people say about their neighbors when it turns out that they are notorious drug-dealers or even axe murderers. TV reporters are often sent out to question neighbors about the villains in notorious cases and even if someone has been caught with bodies buried in his basement, invariably some of the neighbors will say they find it hard to believe that Joe, Sam or Willie could be a murderer. They invariably say such things as; "He has always been such a nice, quiet fellow," or "I still don't believe that Sam could do something like that."

Probably if they'd spent more time with their neighbor, they would have developed a different take but the little time that most of us spend talking to our neighbors leads to us having the equivalent of a long-term second impression of them.

A GOOD FIRST IMPRESSION OFTEN LEADS TO A GOOD SECOND IMPRESSION

If you make a good first impression and do not destroy it when you are conversing with the person or persons you just met, that first impression will solidify into a good second impression, which will almost always become a permanent impression. The problem is that eighty to ninety percent of us destroy, or at least weaken, our good first impression within twenty-five minutes of our initial meeting. The most common way we do so is by greeting someone with a warm, friendly smile and then quickly displaying a bland, or worse, angry or unhappy expression. People are forced to ask themselves which is the real you, the smiling person or the aggressive annoyed one. Most people will decide your smile was a fake. Unfortunately, if people send a mixed positive and negative message, an overwhelming majority will be convinced the negative persona is the real person.

This does not mean that you should force yourself to keep a smile on your face from the beginning to the end of a first meeting. As I wrote earlier, wearing a grin on your face for too long creates for most the impression that you're a slick phony. After about five minutes, no matter the situation, you should settle into a look of friendly and genuinely interested attention. If you do this for ten or fifteen minutes, you will most often create a good second impression.

FOLLOWING A FIRST NON-IMPRESSION

As discussed in the last section many people make little or no first impression when they meet others for the first time. At one time I thought that meant they had a blank slate for a next meeting, but that proved true only when there was a significant gap in time between a first and second encounter. If their next interaction is part of an ongoing relationship or the second meeting takes place shortly after the first, those who make no impression are in the same position as people who make a poor first impression. Not only does a poor second impression outweigh a good first impression but a wishy-washy second impression will not only destroy a good first impression it will create a terrible negative second impression. A weak second impression unless corrected usually lasts a lifetime.

To correct a weak first or second impression, you must be decidedly positive in your next encounter. The best way to do this is to pretend that you haven't met the person before and really work at making a good first impression.

SECOND IMPRESSIONS FOLLOW FIRST IMPRESSIONS WITHIN MINUTES

In our research, we found that those who kill their chances of being popular during an initial meeting, usually do that in the fifth and sixth minutes of the encounter. This is the juncture, we discovered, at which people start to form a second impression. It is also the critical transition period when most people relax and become their natural or real selves.

Popular people change their demeanor less at this critical juncture than most of us. Their smiles are usually not as bright and exuberant, often becoming only a hint of a smile but they still come across as friendly, warm and upbeat. Similarly, they may not hold themselves quite as erect but their posture remains good. If you very carefully watch people when they first meet at a party or business function, in some cases you will clearly see this shift take place. Doing so will help you to keep in mind that you must not allow yourself to fall into the trap of making such a dramatic change.

SECOND IMPRESSIONS ARE LARGELY ABOUT CONVERSATION STYLE

While first impressions are formed mainly by nonverbal signals, second impressions are influenced by the substance of what you say and your conversational style.

Good conversations follow well established, if generally unspoken, rules. It is vital not to talk non-stop; talented conversationalists are sure to give those they are talking to, plenty of opportunity to join in the conversation. They make sure to ask the people they are talking to their views on the subject under discussion. When someone is talking they never interrupt particularly in the middle of a sentence, and they almost always give others the chance to finish a thought. Keep in mind that it's more important if you wish to be popular to become a great listener than a great talker, and it is easier.

REREAD THE ABOVE PARAGRAPH

There are exceptions to the don't interrupt rule. For example, at a contentious business meeting, if a subject is being discussed on which you think that your point of view should be represented you probably should interrupt. You can also interrupt at a social gathering if you think someone is misrepresenting you or your organization. There are of course other occasions when you should interrupt but whether you interrupt or not is a judgement call. As a general rule you should never interrupt a speaker but if you do try to do so without being rude and without hurting people's feelings. Women tend to be more forgiving of others who break in with a point, or even a new topic, as long as that's part of an interesting exchange. However, if a woman cuts another off in a dismissive manner, it can and often does destroy a good first or second impression. Interrupting is often annoying so if you can avoid it, do.

SPEAK SMOOTHLY AND WITHOUT HESITATION

Another feature of conversational style that contributes to making a good second impression is speaking with assurance, without "ums" or off-point digressions. Popular people, particularly popular businessmen and executives, almost always move and speak without hesitating. When we train salespeople, we tell them when they walk into a buyer's office to move right up to his desk and when they speak, to speak clearly and unhesitatingly. Keep in mind that hesitating is not the same as pausing. When you pause purposely, you convey unhurried self-assurance and thoughtfulness. Hesitation, by contrast, can make you look nervous, and it is generally looked upon as a sign of insecurity or ineptitude. Any nervous mannerism, such as shifting in your chair, or shifting your weight from one foot to the other, will be off-putting and send the message that you are unsure of yourself and or unsure of what you're saying. This will cause some people who normally would accept you to dislike and distrust you. Obviously, that would destroy any positive message you sent earlier.

The difference between pausing and hesitating is a matter of style and control. An effective pause lasts only for a few seconds, after which the speaker continues without hesitation and without repeating or getting off-track.

GRACEFUL CONFIDENCE

The power of smooth unhesitating speech is only one way of helping to create a strong positive impression. The grace with which people carry themselves sends the signal that they are self-assured, which as we discussed in the last section, is one of the key elements of being popular. This is one of the reasons that high school athletes are often more popular than non-athletes, even later in life when they are out of shape. The techniques they use to control their movements learned when playing sports stays with them, and this is true for both men and women. In our work we also found both male and female students were more graceful if they took dance lessons. So engaging in activities that require grace and control of movement is a great way to improve your first and second impressions.

RESPECTING THE PERSONAL SPACE OF OTHERS

One of the ways that popular people display respect for others is they are sensitive to personal territorial boundaries. They seldom invade another's personal space unless they are invited to do so. Standing too close when in conversation is only the most obvious violation of space. If you sit across from a businessperson at a restaurant half the table is yours. However, if you sit in front of that same person's desk, your personal space does not extend to the middle of the desk. If you're sitting at the side or in front of someone's desk and you want to put papers on the part of the desk right in front of you, it's wise to ask permission before doing so. Some people will not object to your doing that but although they usually don't say anything, a substantial percentage will. As a general rule, you should never go around to the other side of a person's desk unless they ask you or you have asked permission.

It's also important to understand that men and women have a different sense of personal space. The amount of personal space they need to be comfortable is different. Women tend to stand closer when they first meet someone. The distance at which women feel comfortable in conversation is about six to eight inches closer than that at which men are comfortable. So, if you are a man meeting a woman, in most cases you should stand just a bit closer than you normally do. That will put her at ease. If you are a woman speaking to a man, and you stay at the distance that makes you feel comfortable, you will sometimes find the man backing away. We saw this over and over when we videotaped saleswomen selling to men. Big, tough macho males will never admit that a woman getting too close makes them feel uncomfortable, but, in fact, it does. If you find a man you are speaking to is backing away, you must back off. Doing so will put him at ease. Similarly, if you are a man talking to a woman and you stand the distance at which you feel comfortable, she will see you as cold and distant. You have to move in just a bit.

MAINTAINING UNDIVIDED ATTENTION

Another way to maintain a good first impression, and solidify a positive second impression, is to focus your attention on the person with whom you are interacting, particularly when they are speaking. Paying careful attention to the people with whom you are interacting can make that person feel special. The first and most important step is to look directly at the person who is speaking and under no circumstances let yourself be distracted. In addition, you must enthusiastically partake in any conversation, even if you barely speak. You can actively participate without saying a word, by nodding, leaning forward, looking intently at the speaker, all of which clearly convey that you are listening, and in most cases agreeing with what is being said. Or you can make brief comments such as "uh huh," "yes, I agree." Nodding in agreement can also be very effective. I often noted that both Nancy Reagan and Hillary Clinton would regularly nod their heads in agreement when their husbands were giving a speech or an interview. My wife called them bobble heads, thinking they looked silly. But giving their husbands such supportive attention generally played well for them on TV. They knew what they were doing.

Keeping one's attention riveted can be tricky. When we trained business people to do this, they generally made two mistakes. One was that they stared too intently at the person they were meeting, making him or her uncomfortable. When we told them to ease off a bit, most corrected this mistake easily. The second more serious mistake was that they lost their concentration within a few minutes. They began shifting their bodies, fidgeting, breaking eye contact, and even looking around the room when the other person was speaking. That destroyed any good impression they made and in most cases it was the 'Kiss of death' to their chances of becoming popular.

REREAD THE ABOVE PARAGRAPH

Most often when we look around or look away when someone is speaking, we don't intend to offend; our minds simply wander. You might ask, as my students have hundreds of times, "If my mind wanders, how will anyone know? The fact is that it's usually obvious, so obvious that a seasoned speaker can just glance into a large audience and spot those not paying attention.

IMITATE POPULARITY SUPERSTARS

It will help you understand the importance of giving your undivided attention to the people you meet if you know how the two best known popularity superstars in American politics Ronald Reagan and Bill Clinton treated people. When we interviewed people who met both men, before or during their presidencies, they said; "He made me feel like the center of his universe," or something similar. Even those who disagreed with them politically, including outright political enemies, who were usually hard-boiled professional politicians, said they liked them at the end of the meeting. As hard as they tried and as much as they wanted to, they couldn't deny the charm of these two. Of course, the fact that they gave people such undivided attention even when they held such a powerful position intensified the effect, and for most of us, doing so isn't going to create that off-the-charts result. However, it will definitely seal the deal on a good second impression.

Because maintaining such attention for an extended period is so difficult for so many people, we developed a technique for teaching students to do so. We told them to pretend the person they are meeting is going to become their best friend or at least someone who will be very important to them in the future. This is a very effective technique because it stopped my students from becoming angry or annoyed when the person they were talking to said something that struck them as stupid or banal. Most of us would never do that to a close friend or someone we thought was going to become a close friend.

ASK FRIENDLY QUESTIONS TO PUT THEM AT EASE

We found that naturally popular people tend to have genuine interest in others. They enjoy meeting new people and learning about them. This is why when popular people meet someone they tend to ask the person a number of questions about him or herself. They seem to do this instinctively, even when they don't realize that they are doing it, they almost always study people they meet. I've found that most popular people are keen observers and their ability to understand others is one of the things that gives them a tremendous advantage in their business and social lives. I discovered this as part of a study I conducted on whether popular people remember the names of those they meet better than most of us. At some time, we have all forgotten the name of someone we've just met, which can be embarrassing, especially if you are then joined by someone you know and good manners requires you to introduce them to the person you just met. I expected that popular people would be better at remembering names. So I ran a little survey in which I asked people I had identified as popular, average, and unpopular to recall the names of people they had recently met at parties. I was surprised to discover that not only did popular people generally know the names of those they had met for just a few minutes but also knew quite a bit about them.

I found that when Joe and Jane average talked to someone for five to ten minutes, two hours later they usually remembered little or nothing about the person, whereas popular people knew something about almost everyone they met. They often had information about the personal lives of those they just met. What amazed me was they were ready and willing to make comments about the personalities of people they hardly knew. They said such things as, "Oh, Tom, he's not too sure of himself." or "Tom seems very confident." "He really knows what he's doing and seems on top of his game." Even when they knew only a few facts about people, they were often right on target in their assessments. They weren't right all the time, but even when they were wrong, it was obvious they had asked a few questions and had paid careful attention to the answers.

A LITTLE ABOUT REMEMBERING NAMES

All my life I've had difficulty remembering names. That is why over the years I have read countless articles on the subject. Many of them said even if you have a history of forgetting names you must convince yourself you can learn to remember them. If you're convinced that you are just no good at remembering names, you will be. If you have a normal memory, the reason you don't remember names is you never made it a priority and as result you do not pay careful attention when you are introduced. Paying careful attention to someone's name when you're introduced is essential if you're going to remember their name. I did pay attention, in fact I made it a priority but it didn't help that much.

My wife and I for years ate dinner in front of the television and watched the news. About a year-and-a-half ago we stopped doing that because the news consisted of politicians insulting each other and we found that so depressing, we switched to watching a comedy channel. A few months later they added a show called "The Last Man Standing." It was about a right-wing guy with a wife and three daughters. Like most TV comedies it was occasionally funny so we watched it. Three or four weeks later the show introduced a new character. I did not think the bit was funny but my wife thought it was hilarious. When I asked what's so funny she said don't you recognize her she was his wife on the last show he had. The minute she mentioned it I remembered the show, in it he had three sons and apparently some of the jokes depended on the audience knowing that. Since I had not immediately recognized his wife from an earlier show I didn't get the jokes. My wife noticed that and said something that changed my life, you remember the characters on the old show but you don't remember what they looked like. At that point I decided to carefully study the faces of those I met for the first time. Once I did that half my problem was solved. The minute I started studying people's faces I started remembering their names. What was more I started noticing when they were in a good mood or in a bad mood and particularly when they were upset. Almost instantly I had an advantage when dealing with people I had not had before.

As you know when I run across a new problem I research it. When we questioned people who said they had difficulty remembering names, they were as likely to have difficulty remembering faces. After further study I decided that many people who think they don't remember names, really don't remember faces. This is a bigger problem for men than it is for women, but both reported that once they started studying faces they were more likely to remember names. Therefore, it is necessary to carefully study faces when you are being introduced. Since you can't stare at people or you'll make them uncomfortable, you should attempt to study their faces without them knowing you're doing it. As we discussed earlier, going over the person's face right to left or from left to right is an excellent way to study them, without the person becoming upset or uncomfortable. However, since popular people give their undivided attention to those they meet they automatically study and remember faces.

Since I have difficulty remembering names I handed the research on remembering faces over to one of my researchers. He found if you have this problem and you examine carefully the faces of everyone you meet, you will dramatically increase your chances of remembering the faces of those you have just met. Apparently people get better at remembering faces after they practice for two or three weeks. The best way of doing this is when you're in a bus, a train, a restaurant or any other place where people gather, pick one person and cross over his face. Then close your eyes and see if you can picture that person. If not, cross over again and try again. Limit yourself to two crossovers per person. Choose a second person and do the same. Once you are able to create a picture in your mind of almost anyone you meet, try two at a time.

You can practice remembering faces almost anywhere and at any time. The reason I say almost is I know a woman who had worked as a nurse in the emergency room. She said she regularly treated people who fell down stairs, walked into walls, were hit by cars or trucks because they were texting as they walked, drove etc. Don't try studying faces as you walk down the street, or at any other time when it will distract you from the world around you.

For those who cannot remember names the standard advice given by almost everyone is valid. When you're introduced repeat the person's name as soon as possible and repeat it as often as you can without being awkward. Start by repeating the name when you're introduced. Repeat the name to confirm it's pronunciation or that you heard it. Another way of using a person's name is to ask a question. Mary, in what department do you work? Tom, where do you come from originally? Another technique suggested by several experts was to bring someone over and introduce Mary to them, or someone to Mary. I'm sure you can think of dozens more. Even after you are convinced you know the person's name end the conversation by using it once more.

Many experts also advise their followers to form a memorable picture in their minds to help them remember a name. That can be very useful but it also can be very tricky and very embarrassing. When I taught in high school the physics teacher wanted his new students to know the names of those physicists who changed the world. So before his first quiz he told them he would ask them to name the world's greatest physicist. One of his students answer was A Beer and while correcting his test in the teachers room he asked aloud where in the world did he get that answer? When I said that he probably formed the picture in his mind of someone in Germany with a stein in his hand asking for a beer. He couldn't believe it so he sent for the student who confirmed my theory. He said he was thinking of "eine stein." We all laughed and he gave the student 1point of 3 for his creativity. However, I don't think the student would've done as well if he had been in Einstein's class and called him Professor Beer. I don't recommend this method because of the possibility of silly embarrassing mistakes.

While it's always important to remember the names of people you met sometimes it is critical. If the people you just met work in your office or your company and you know you are going to be interacting with them in the near future and your career will be affected by the impression you make you must try harder. On those occasions it would be wise to write the names down and if possible take a number of pictures with these people in the background. Then when you get home match the pictures with the names and study them. When you meet them don't count on them remembering you, introduce yourself and remind them that you met them at the Christmas party. This will create a favorable impression because everyone likes to be one of those you remember.

REREAD A LITTLE ABOUT REMEMBERING NAMES 2X. IF YOU HAVE A PROBLEM REMEMBERING NAMES 5X

WHEN THEY ARE NOT TALKING

What do you do if someone you meet doesn't strike up a conversation with you, and just sits or stands quietly? The first rule is if he or she doesn't speak after a short time, you must. Do not start by bringing up a subject chosen specifically to show how intelligent or knowledgeable you are. Try to get the person you just met to tell you about his expertise or her interest. If they're not forthcoming ask questions about his or her work and hobbies. Areas about which the person you just met can probably speak fluently and possibly show off just a bit.

The best way to create the impression you are a friendly person when you first meet is to put them at ease. Get them talking by asking non-confrontational, non-threatening questions. This works particularly well with people who are not outgoing and very seldom start conversations themselves. However, if you once engage them in conversation in which they can contribute most will think of you as a friend.

STOP & GLANCE

Popular people steer conversations to subjects on which they think they will have an instant rapport with the other person. Charmers hardly ever talk about religion or politics; they usually stick to subjects that are light and non-confrontational. They never argue with those they just met. In fact, they hardly ever argue with anyone. Popular people tend to talk about subjects that others find interesting. If they know the person is a sports fan, a golfer, a sailor or an opera buff they will steer the conversation to that subject. When they have no idea what people like they ask them about their favorite books, restaurants, movies, actors, and so forth.

One of the most successful ways to get a good conversation going is to ask complementary questions, such as: Where did you get that beautiful dress?" or "I hear you're a good golfer."

For men, sports is one of the most popular topics of conversation and if you know little or nothing about sports, whether you are a man or a woman, you are at a tremendous disadvantage in many social and business gatherings. Make an effort to keep up with the local teams, so that you can intelligently discuss what's going on. This will give you a topic that is non-confrontational and friendly. You don't have to become an expert. As long as you have basic information you can carry on a conversation. Business women should avoid discussing fashion, children or similar feminine subjects when men are present. Those topics make some men very uncomfortable.

Seeking common ground is not only choosing subjects in which almost everyone is interested but also ones about which the other person can contribute. I think the best example I've ever seen was an attorney at a meeting in Chicago. He took my course on selling to juries, but he certainly didn't need it. When we broke for lunch a woman attorney mentioned that she grew up in a Polish area of Chicago. The minute she said that, he told her he visited Chicago all the time and heard about the great restaurants in the Polish section of the city but could never find one. She immediately named half a dozen restaurants, where they were located and their specialties. Being a charmer, he hung on every word, in fact he took notes. The search for common ground is commonly used by experts to put people at ease, stroke their egos and put them in a good mood. Always remember: popular people are popular not because they look good but because they make others look and feel good.

The best way to learn to make good second impressions is to practice with a partner, attending several social or social business gatherings with him or her. Ideally, you're both learning, you should take turns acting as coach and student. Being a coach under these circumstances can be tricky, but you'll learn as much from coaching as from being coached. You have to expect that when you tell anyone, even a good friend, that the way they hold their facial muscles sends a negative message, they will not be overjoyed. Our experience shows that those who have been criticized usually question what is being said. They will say such things as, "I am positive I do not do that." " I do not act that way." "I have bad habits, but that is not one of them," "You mean when I sat down I frowned? Do I really look as if I have lost my best friend?" Don't let this scuttle the process. If your partner takes umbrage this way, let him or her vent. Generally people come to recognize the validity of your concerns once the moment is over.

If a popularity partner objects to what you said don't argue. And whatever you do, do not insist that you are right. You should say that you could be mistaken, but that you're doing your best to help. It usually helps if you point out that he or she is about to judge you as well, and that you may not like or agree with what they tell you either. Often that ends the argument. that is one of the reasons I have students taking turns acting as student and coach.

It is another reason that videotaping is so important. Once people see themselves doing the very things you have pointed out, they almost always try to stop. Role playing is one of the best ways to correct flaws if you videotape yourself as you are doing it. Start by walking over to an imaginary person and placing yourself in a position that respects his territory, then, start talking. Using people you know as characters in your role-playing makes it more realistic and effective. Keep in mind your posture, display a positive attitude, maintain your attention, and keep your movements graceful. When you examine the videotape, most of the time, your mistakes will pop right out at you. Once they do you will want to practice correcting them.

It is very helpful if you practice when you are at work, with strangers in a social setting and socializing with friends. If any time during a conversation you say or imply anything negative, immediately make a mental note and if possible a real note of what you have said. If you hesitated, slouched, or lost your concentration while someone is speaking, you should role-play a scenario, if possible that night, in which you do everything right. If you repeat it at least five times for the next several days you are much less likely to repeat the same mistake. In fact many found when they were about to make a similar mistake a role-playing scenario popped into their minds and they avoided it.

Work on one mistake at a time, and don't overdo it; take a break every fifteen to twenty minutes. If you are working with a partner, it usually works best if you change from student to coach or visa versa approximately every twenty minutes.

STOP & GLANCE

These exercises will take you from one to three hours to complete, and they will help you correct most of your mistakes. If you are not able to correct your mistakes repeat the role playing exercises. We all have poor habits that are so ingrained they take longer to correct than others. Keep at it. If it still is not working vary your approach. When you are stuck take a break and come back to that problem later. If you still can't get it to work, you may be forced to make critical decisions about how to proceed but do not rush them. I suggest that you take a few days off and re-examine your video. If you don't get a new insight and have no idea how to proceed ask a friend or a partner to review the video with you. If that doesn't work start over and redo your videos. Making a good second impression for some will be the most difficult part of becoming popular. It is critical to your success. If you have difficulty mastering any part of making a good second impression try, try, and try again. Sooner or later you will succeed; almost everybody does.

Making a good second impression is so important that I suggest you reread this section. If you are one of those people, who learns things quickly and then performs what you learned with ease and grace and you're not having any difficulty making a good second impression you do not have to read it carefully. You can skim through it, because you'll remember most of it from the first reading. Nevertheless, you should go through it a second time. If you are still having difficulty, read it aloud in front of a mirror, more than once and during the reading stop and practice. Keep in mind becoming popular depends less on talent than determination. Never quit. Sooner or later you will become noticeably more popular.

ASSIGNMENT

Replay tapes if necessary.

*   *   *   *   *   *   *   *   *   *   *   *

Join or start a popularity club that meets with other popularity clubs because it is the first step to power, popularity and success.

SECTION 5

LONG TERM INSTINCTIVE POPULARITY

After working on the exercises many of you will notice that strangers you meet are generally friendlier. Your life will already have started to become more pleasant. You will probably also have received a few negative reactions from people you've known for years. You may have sensed them thinking, "Who do you think you are? What is this act you are putting on?" Some may even have expressed these thoughts out loud. Don't worry. As I wrote earlier, such reactions are normal, and in most cases these friends and family members will in time accept the new, friendlier, better you.

What you do need to be concerned about is slipping back into old bad habits. Sadly, we are all creatures of habit, and unless we keep practicing, we will almost surely revert to those old ways. The good news is that you don't have to work as hard as you did when you started or much longer.

The secret to long term popularity is additional monitoring and practicing after having finished your training. A substantial percentage of our students told us in follow up interviews and reports that after a while, they no longer had to think about most of the changes they had to make in order to send positive messages, though they usually had to watch out for one or two recurring mistakes. Standing up straight, leaning in when they first met someone, pausing for a moment to allow people to settle in before they start talking, holding on just a fraction of a second longer when shaking hands, giving people the appropriate amount of personal space, listening carefully to what others say, asking them questions about themselves and their interests – the full gamut of popularity skills become semi-automatic.

A majority of these successful students told us that they developed a standard sequence of actions which help them to appear friendly. For example, from the minute they said hello, they would automatically stand straighter, begin to smile a bit, and make eye contact. They really didn't have to think about it, they just did it.

REREAD ABOVE TWO PARAGRAPHS 2X

In addition to creating such standard drills for yourself, it's important that you continue monitoring. If you let an old negative signal take over after weeks or months, it can be almost like starting anew. You must continue to monitor and correct.

STOP & GLANCE

The most effective way of doing that is to keep videotaping yourself, or having someone videotape you periodically and at random times during the day. Ideally, you should not know when the tapes are being made, and if you do know you are being taped, you must make a conscious effort not to correct your mistakes while you are being taped. The tapes should be made both at work and at home, if you have set up a workstation at home be sure to tape there. Before looking at the first of these tapes make a list of the changes in your original presentation that needed improvement. Were you slouching, mumbling, looking angry, and so forth. Have yourself videotaped on a typical day when you're working, walking along the street, interacting with friends or strangers, etc.

When you examine these tapes use the list of your old flaws as a guide but don't limit yourself to that list. When you review the old tapes; it's easy to forget where, when and under what circumstance each tape was taken, so each tape should be labeled.

You should also ask a friend or your spouse to occasionally monitor you without your knowing you are being monitored or taped, preferably at both business and social events. Being monitored by the person you are living with works best if you do not overdo it or comment as it is being done. That can and often does create problems. Don't do or ask them to do anything which might strain the relationship. Set up specific times when you can be observed or do the observing. Stick to it and make sure comments are offered only after the taping. If either party is upset by monitoring, stop. The relationship is more important than the monitoring.

A simple way of monitoring your progress daily is to place several cameras on tripods and several mirrors around your house in which you will regularly catch your image. Our students reported the best places to position them were at the end of hallways, across the dinner table, and to the right or left of the television but you can better choose where they are placed because only you know your normal routine.

PESKY PERSISTENT PROBLEMS

While most of the mistakes you continue to make will be easy to correct a majority of you will invariably discover habits that are particularly difficult to permanently change. For example, if your everyday face announces that you are angry or disgruntled and that look just keeps coming up in the tapes, then you will have to practice as long as it takes to eliminate that recurring problem. The best way to correct these persistent problems is to role-play scenarios in front of a mirror while you are being videotaped. You must immediately review the tape after you've completed a few scenarios, and then repeat the exercise and review the tape again. You should repeat this exercise, every day, until you have solved your problem. Then check once a week to make sure you're not slipping. You will probably find that you are, and you'll likely have to repeat this whole procedure, over and over until your problem disappears.

Backsliding often happens with problems that seemed to be easily solved. For example, if you slouch in your chair when you are working, you will probably learn quickly to sit up straight most of the time but bad posture often comes back to haunt people. This is why you should keep videotaping yourself even after the three month period is up; I advise once every three months you videotape yourself for a couple of days and examine the tapes. It's best if you don't videotape yourself on Monday, Tuesday and Wednesday of the same week but on three days about a week apart.

YOU DO NOT HAVE TO BE ALWAYS "ON"

Many students have expressed doubts about how realistic it is to always be so upbeat and attentive to others and as I wrote before some people object to this kind of behavior training because they think it produces fake popularity. So let me address this and similar issues.

First, these skills are not entirely natural even for most popular people. For true popularity superstars, they do seem to be instinctive, even compulsive. In fact, I believe that many of the real charmers have little or no choice in the matter. They desperately need to get everyone to love them. The two classic examples, once again, are Ronald Reagan and Bill Clinton. It's been said of both that if they walked into a room and found ninety-nine people who were on their side and one who was not, they would head straight for the one who was not their friend to win him or her over. Some people will go out of their way to charm even those they don't like or with whom they do not wish to associate. But they are charmers by nature and cannot help themselves or they enjoy charming people so much it becomes almost a game.

Most popular people turn on the charm when it's in their best interest, not all the time. When they interact with someone a dozen times a day, they don't try to charm that person each and every time. Their message is most often a neutral one. But research also shows that popular people do make sure to occasionally smile and look upbeat when they are dealing with people they spend their lives around. They are like most of the top salespeople we studied; they can turn their charm off and on at will. Interestingly, some of the most popular people I have run across were not likable all the time; they were charming only when they wanted to be.

While popularity superstars like Clinton and Reagan seem to come by their popularity skills naturally, for most charming people their skills are the result of a combination of instinct and intellect. They send the right messages in large part because they have trained themselves to do so or their environment when they were growing up or even in college or business conditioned them to be charming. They are aware of what makes them popular and they fully realize and are proud of the fact that they're able to turn on their charm at will.

Learning these skills should not be considered "faking it." You're simply teaching yourself skills that others have picked up by accident, perhaps by copying popular parents or friends, or being taught by them, or by close observation. Most children pick up the nonverbal signals they send for the rest of their lives before they are two. If you're one of them and almost everyone is, the signals you habitually send are so ingrained that you will never completely eliminate them but you can and you should when necessary adjust and refine them.

This doesn't mean that those who are naturally popular don't have some additional qualities that are products of their personalities that we would all do well to emulate. If you are interested in continuing to deepen your popularity over time, there are two important skills that you should try to cultivate.

READING PEOPLE

First, you must learn to read people. One of the characteristics of popular people is they respond to subtle signals given off by those with whom they are interacting. Popular people read others so well they have the ability to sense when someone is in a bad mood or something is bothering them. This is one of the main reasons these people sustain their popularity throughout their lives; they are usually gentle and understanding when they see that something is bothering someone they know.

You can teach yourself to become better at this. In one class, I instructed the students to pay careful attention to the people they met and asked them to write a short description of each new acquaintance. As they read their sketches I was struck by the fact that they included not only descriptions of their looks and behavior, but an analysis of their characters and moods. When I asked them how they developed this information, those with the most detailed descriptions said they had watched the people carefully. To read people, they claimed, all they had to do was to pay careful attention to them, to what they said and how they said it.

I decided to test whether the sales people we were working with also did this. I put a couple of questions in several surveys, and to my surprise and delight, top salespeople said they studied buyers all the time. Once we instructed average and below-average salespeople to study their buyers this way, their sales increased and they seemed to build a better rapport with some of their buyers. In addition, we discovered that when we told people to study those they interacted with in social settings, it also worked wonders by improving the impressions they made.

REREAD ABOVE TWO PARAGRAPHS 2X

Up to this point I have talked about making a good or poor first and second impression. I did so because I am using the terminology everyone uses and the reading public recognizes. However, there are degrees of good and poor impressions. Earlier I discussed making very poor first impressions. I explained how some people turn everyone off before they say a word. I would like to point out at this juncture that there are some charmers who are so effective that people literally look upon them as friends five minutes after they have met them. There are others who are treated like popularity superstars after meeting people for just a few minutes. The one thing they have in common is they read people very well.

Earlier I pointed out that many people if they carefully study those with whom they interact, cannot only figure out their personalities but predict with uncanny accuracy how they will react in different situations. They not only watch them when they first meet them but study them as their relationship develops. After a relatively short period of careful observation most of us can figure out what it is that will get certain individuals to react positively to us and our suggestions.

We tested this theory with a number of students. We told them to carefully study those they just met and those they had known for a long time. With that simple instruction, within a week or two our students saw improvements in their ability to charm others. In addition, a substantial percentage of mothers who instructed their young children who were having problems getting along with others to watch their popular playmates reported their children were making friends more easily and as a result had more friends. The younger the children the more effective this technique but it helped with most children and a substantial percentage of adults.

DON'T RAISE POPULAR CHILDREN RAISE POPULAR ADULTS

The best time to start training your children is in their second year in Junior High School. If your daughter asks for the book a year or two earlier give it to her, girls mature sooner than boys and she can probably handle it. There are two reasons for starting at this time; first popularity becomes important to them at that point and they are more likely to do the work necessary to become popular and second working with this text will teach them how to be more popular in their group. Which is very important because that is the one element of high school popularity that carries into adulthood.

Youngsters in Junior High and High School divide themselves into groups, some groups are popular while others are not. If your son or daughter is not in a popular group you might wish to help but that's generally a waste of time, at their age being good looking, engaging in a popular activity eg. cheer leading or playing football and wearing or carrying the current status items in their school are the keys to social success. As most of you already know which group they belong to in High School is not a factor once they become adults. What is important is how popular they are within their own group, that is the best predictor of how popular they will be as adults. So teaching them to charm members of their group will increase their chances of social, sexual and business success as adults.

Girls are twice as likely to take this book seriously, while most of the boys will put off starting or only give certain sections a try. Don't let that happen.

One of the most successful ways to encourage young people to work on their popularity skills is to point out to them that once they develop a pleasant demeanor it will not only affect those they deal with but those they pass in the hallways or meet elsewhere. This is significant because if they meet these people in another setting they are more likely to be remembered because people remember those they like. If you have ever known a really popular person when they walk into a party, a meeting, or a bar they seem to know people. These people are not their close friends just acquaintances who they met once or twice. After being popular for a few years you will have friends almost everywhere you go. You will not only enjoy the experience of meeting people you know, you will also enjoy the experience of being seen as one of those popular people. At that point everyone will want to be your friend.

The reason I wrote this section on raising popular children is whenever I spoke on the subject of popularity I was surrounded by adults who wanted to help their children. Encouraging your children to start before 13 or 14 is counterproductive. Don't do it, don't do it, please don't do it,

I do not recommend that teenagers practice reading other teens faces, what we tell them is to carefully observe their most popular friends. Young people naturally imitate those they admire and they usually are very good at it. Let them work at becoming popular in their own way. Your primary job as parents is to remind them over and over that how popular or unpopular they are in junior high and High School does not count once they become adults. In fact we all know people who are loved by everyone who couldn't possibly have been popular in high school and others who belonged to the in group who are now the butt of jokes. This is useful information not only for those who are unpopular as kids but those who are popular and think their high school popularity will last forever. Unless they develop real popularity skills, it will not.

BULLYING

If your youngster is being bullied in school often there is very little he or she can do about it. It is your job as a parent to put a stop to it. Your first step should be to visit the principal and insist that he stop it immediately. If he ignores you I suggest you ask your child and other children at his school to name other children who are being bullied. Believe me they will know. Once you find out who they are contact their parents and then arrange to visit the principal as a group. That should solve your problem, if not you have to do whatever it takes to make your child feel safe and secure in school.

Believe it or not the real victims of bullying are the bullies. If a bully is accused and the accusation becomes part of his or her school record few colleges will accept them. Because most parents do not believe their children are or even could be bullies, they don't warn them about the possibility they can ruin their lives if they become directly or indirectly involved in bullying. There's a real possibility your son's or daughter's life can be destroyed just because they want to go along with the in crowd. A substantial percentage of schools today have zero tolerance for bullying and that's a good thing but it's also a trap. I looked into a number of cases where youngsters who did not personally do the bullying encouraged others to become part of a crowd that was bullying someone. Before your youngster goes to middle school explain to them that being bullied can ruin the lives of those being bullied but it's more likely to ruin the lives of those doing the bullying. Sit them down and in no uncertain terms tell them that if they're ever involved in that kind of activity you will punish them severely, take away their computer, cell phone and anything else that means anything to them. Make sure they understand you are deadly serious. I repeat bullying can and does ruin lives. However, if your youngster works at improving his or her popularity skills they will never bully anyone, it's not the way to become popular.

GET YOUR CHILD'S PASSWORD

If you're a parent and you do not have the password to your child's cell phone you're not doing your job. Teenagers today cannot have a right to privacy. If you do not have the password to your son's or daughter's cell phone etc. you are making a dangerous mistake. If you have a son you should know his password because if he's being bullied he probably will not tell you and if he's doing the bullying that's even worse. I also ran across several cases where young men went to meet young girls and found they were 45 year old perverts and although that doesn't happen very often, it does happen. Of course you want to know if your daughter is being bullied and believe it or not a majority of them do not tell their parents. And if your sweet little girl is part of a group that is doing the bullying, it will come as a shock to you but by that time it will be too late. In today's politically correct colleges her application will not even be read. In addition, today young girls often send pictures to their boyfriends that no one would want made public. When they break up with that boy some of the boys will send those pictures to their friends and once they're out there it's almost impossible to get them back. They can embarrass your daughter even as an adult. However, that's not the main reason you must have your daughters password without going into details there are literally thousands of cases of young girls who thought they were communicating with people their age and found out later they were not. Horrible things happen to those young girls and some of their bodies are never found. Don't be your daughter's friend, be her parent. Protect her online, it's a very dangerous place.

OBSERVING AND ANALYZING THOSE YOU MEET

As I said, being able to read people is absolutely essential to social and business success, therefore we must all work at developing this skill, which will take more work for men than for women. Women are generally more observant than men, though some women also lack this skill. If you have any doubts about your ability to read people you must work at learning how to do so. You can start with your friends, your loved ones, your boss, your coworkers, and your subordinates. I suggested earlier that you carefully study popular waiters in restaurants to pick up the messages they send and how they send them. You will find that if you study those in your daily life in a similar way, you will pick up on the visual and verbal cues they send all the time and you will become more adept at identifying people's moods. As I pointed out earlier, very popular people read other people's moods and are very kind and gentle when others seem depressed or upset. In addition, you will learn when they want to talk and when they'd rather not and when they've found something you've said amusing or offensive. This will dramatically improve your chance of charming others. Most executives we spoke to agreed being able to charm people when necessary is an essential business skill.

DAN THE MAN COLLINS

One of the most impressive examples of masterful people reading skills I have witnessed was on a sales call with one of the most popular salespeople I ever ran across, "Dan the man Collins." That was the way he introduced himself and he lived up to his name. He was a big energetic fellow who smiled the minute he met a client. I accompanied him on about twenty sales calls as part of my research. The reason I spent so much time with him was that in a business where most sales people made a sale on a call less than thirty percent of the time, he sold almost everyone he met. He did so most of the time without being intimidating or aggressive, though if his considerable charm didn't do the trick, he was tenacious. Once he started selling it was almost impossible to get rid of him, he hung on like a bulldog. In spite of this, most of his clients didn't like him they loved him.

On our second day together, he received a call from the home office. Word was out that one of the biggest potential clients in the state was looking around for a new supplier. The minute he heard that he called to make an appointment and when her secretary said the woman would be willing to see him that afternoon, he practically danced. He told me that he had been waiting for this opportunity for years. The decision-maker was a woman in her mid-fifties who intimidated most of his competitors, but not him. He knew her well, he had sold to her when he worked for another company. In less than twenty minutes, we were in a cab heading for her office. When we got there, he jumped out of the taxi grinning from ear to ear and said: "If you want to know how to sell, watch me today."

We were almost instantly ushered into the buyer's office. But as we walked through the door, he took one look at her, put his hand on my shoulder, pushed me toward the door, and said, "John, wait for me outside." I did as instructed, but since her door was not completely closed I positioned myself so I could see and hear the sales presentation. To my shock the first words out of his mouth were, "You are in no mood to listen to a sales presentation, I will come back another time. I do not know what's bothering you, but if it will help to talk about it, I'll listen." When we left the office fifteen minutes later, I asked why he did not even try to sell to her. Dan explained that he could see she was in a terrible mood, and he did not think there was any point making a presentation.

Over the next several years as I studied one top salesperson after another, most of whom had the tenacity of pit bulls, I saw many of them call off sales presentations because the buyer was upset or, in his or her opinion, in no mood to buy. Interestingly, while over eighty percent of the top salespeople in corporations were men, most of the salespeople who canceled presentations for this reason were women, which should not be surprising given that women are generally more empathetic. What did surprise my researchers was that although top salesmen were often macho guys, they acted very much like the top saleswomen when they were dealing with prospects.

We taped these sales presentations whenever possible so that we could study them. When we looked at the tapes we could see these salesmen studying and analyzing the buyers to get a good read on their mood. That is why today many of the more sophisticated trainers work at making salesmen more sensitive to their buyers.

FEELING GOOD ABOUT YOURSELF

The other key characteristics of naturally popular people is they like and respect themselves, they stand up for themselves and demand that others respect them. This came as a surprise to many in my popularity classes because they assumed that I would be telling them to kiss-up to everyone. They mistakenly believed that to become popular they would have to sacrifice their dignity and integrity. I always enjoyed explaining that just the opposite is true—that to be truly popular they have to maintain their dignity and integrity. Remember, doormat popularity is not real popularity.

When we observed popular men and women from all socioeconomic backgrounds and all sections of this country, we found that they would not allow anyone to disrespect them and they did not disrespect themselves. If they were disrespected or not treated well by anyone no matter who, they would object. Ninety-nine percent of the time they fought back verbally, although over a twenty-five-year period I witnessed three fistfights. Only one resulted in someone being injured, and that was minor. In addition, popular people often fought to maintain their dignity or to protect their reputation even when they knew they were going to lose.

Obviously, respecting yourself and learning to demand that others do can be difficult for some people. This is really beyond the purview of this book, but I will say that by improving your popularity through the techniques I've suggested you are likely to begin feeling better about yourself and gain more confidence to stand up for yourself.

Lifetime popularity is not a gift of the gods. If you want it, you are going to have to work at it, at least for a while. But sooner or later sending the right messages will become as natural to you as breathing and you will turn your charm on and off as easily as you do a light switch. This will come about only if you practice, practice and practice some more. It's like learning to play golf or tennis, you'll have more fun playing the game once you get the basics down but you will always work at improving because that's part of the game.

REREAD THE ABOVE PARAGRAPH

Many of my students found after the initial stages practicing popularity skills was fun. One set of former students who formed a practice group told me that they have continued to meet for years after taking my class not only because it helps them to keep their skills sharp, but because they enjoyed those meetings. In fact, the members of that group have become friends with those in another group. Occasionally, the two groups have lunch together. I attended one of their lunches two years ago and had a great time. They had all learned different popularity skills and at their meetings they talked about using them. These sessions were very enlightening and occasionally very funny. The first group took my class seven years earlier and met on the third Friday of every month and included three members who had never taken my class. The second group had taken the class within the last year and usually got together on short notice because they worked together. The meeting I attended was more a social session than a training session. Both meetings were wonderful. I hope you will someday have such meetings and enjoy them as much as these two friendly and entertaining groups.

However, if you're one of those who have worked diligently and are still not charming most of the people you meet you made one or two mistakes. First, the messages you practiced sending are not the right ones. If you worked by yourself this is likely. You must go back and with the help of others come up with friendly positive messages that you can send consistently. Second, if you've been practicing sending the right signals obviously you have not been able to condition yourself to do so. Start over and this time when you're told to memorize or reread a section of this text reread it in a loud voice in front of a mirror. The more senses you use when conditioning yourself the more effective the conditioning.

If you are in the majority and because of this book you are more popular, happier or more successful I would like you to write to me and tell me about your experience. If you have problems I want you to write me as well and possibly we can solve them together. In fact, I would like you to write to me at several stages of your progress. Tell me if after six months you are getting positive feedback from the public and if it has changed your life. I would like you to write me as well when you finish the training and tell me what impact it had on you and those around you. Based on this information I will up-date the book and publish any new findings online for those who already have the book.

*   *   *   *   *   *   *   *   *   *   *   *

The one thing that has never changed is those who joined popularity clubs were more likely to succeed than those that did not.

I spent twenty seven years researching and writing this book, so of course I want you to succeed because unless you succeed this book will not. If you have reached the end of the book without making substantial progress I beg you to go back and try again because just about everyone in my classes who worked at it after they thought they had failed told me they were not only more popular but happier and more successful. You can be to.

If you are one of the majority who now have the ability to charm most of those you meet I thank you for taking this wonderful journey with me and I wish you nothing but the best. However, I feel obliged to tell you that two-thirds of you after you have attained your goal and are able to charm almost everyone you meet will continue to refine your skills. Like golfers and tennis players improving your game will become an obsession, that's the bad news, the good news is you will enjoy the game.

Because you have put time and effort into this undertaking most of you have succeeded and as a result of your hard work I'm sure this book will become successful.

Thank You,

John T.Molloy